ISBN: 0986256412
ISBN-13: 978-0986256417

The Poetry of Spirituality

AS SEEN THROUGH THE EYES OF A PSYCHOTHERAPIST

ELIZABETH DICKSON, LCSW

CONTENTS

INTRODUCTION   1

AWE

Awe and the Celebration of Life's Mystery   7

Finding the "More" in the Moment   11

The Miracle of Felt Meaning   19

The Spiritual Dimension of Felt Meaning   29

Conclusions: Felt Meaning and Psychotherapy   39

FAITH

What is Faith?   47

The 23rd Psalm as Metaphor   53

Why We Are Not Alone   61

Three Sources of Faith for Psychotherapists   69

Integrating Psychotherapy and Spiritually   77

The Importance of Doubt   83

LOVE

The Confusion About Love   93

Parameters for Unconditional Love   97

A Different Way to Think About Love   105

Love as a Source of Direction   113

The Spiritual Dimension of Love   117

COMPASSION

Compassion as Being Together with Suffering   125

Compassion and Psychotherapy: Joining Versus Fixing   131

The Compassionate Encounter with the Self   137

The Potential for Transformation   145

The Soul Journey: Reframing the Meaning of Suffering   153

JOY AND GRATITUDE

Joy as a Spiritual Emotion   161

The Relationship Between Joy and Gratitude   163

Heeding the Soul's Calling   169

ABOUT THE AUTHOR   177

ACKNOWLEDGEMENTS   179

BIBLIOGRAPHY   181

INTRODUCTION

*Finding Inspiration From Awe, Faith, Love, Compassion,
Joy And Gratitude*

A FRAMEWORK FOR VIEWING SPIRITUALITY

There are few things as important to mankind as the uplifting emotional states that we associate with spirituality; so much of our happiness depends upon how well we can access feelings such as awe, faith, love, compassion, joy and gratitude. And yet it seems, as a culture, that we do not focus enough on these states. We may understand them at some basic level, but have we really explored what they mean to us and how they are evolving for us personally?

I have divided this book into five sections—each dealing with one (or two, in the case of joy and gratitude) of these emotional states, which I will refer to as "spiritual emotions." I am attempting to create a framework for viewing the vast and often confusing subject of spirituality. It follows that, by using spiritual emotions as my framework, I am describing spirituality from an experiential perspective—how it actually ends up feeling to us. What I have chosen to emphasize is ultimately based upon my own subjective experience, but I hope that it will resonate for others as well.

PSYCHOTHERAPY AND SPIRITUALITY

As a psychotherapist, I am also very much aware of how

1

spiritual emotions play out in the psychotherapy process. This topic sparks passion for many (though certainly not all) psychotherapists. But because of the controversy surrounding the word "spiritual," the subject of the spiritual emotions is not generally addressed in our professional settings. So, in addition to exploring these emotional states in a general way, I am also writing about the role that they play in psychotherapy. In doing this, I have two goals in mind. The first is to enhance our understanding of this important dimension of psychotherapy that tends to get ignored. And second, I wish to contribute to our appreciation of the spiritual emotions themselves by offering a different context or lens from which to view them.

BYPASSING THE CONTROVERSY

Hopefully we can bypass some of the controversy about spirituality by thinking of it not as a belief system or a life style commitment, but rather as a source of poetic language. There is something universal about so much of the poetry of spirituality. It has the power to reach us, whether or not we call ourselves religious, believe in a personal God, or even approve of the word "spiritual."

Rather than thinking of therapists as trying to help clients become more spiritual (which is not typically the goal of therapy), we might think of spiritually-oriented therapists as those who are able to cultivate the spiritual emotions in the therapy process in a way that promotes healing and growth for their clients. The point is not whether the client or the therapist consider themselves spiritual, but whether awe, faith, love, compassion, joy or gratitude come alive in the actual therapy sessions. I certainly have had many clients who were quite cynical about spirituality, and yet the spiritual emotions were often alive and thriving in the therapy room.

RESPECTING THE DARK SIDE

This does not mean, however, that spiritually-oriented therapists just value positive emotions. Although my focus is on uplifting emotional states, I do not intend to exclude the darker human emotions, such as loneliness, despair, pain, grief or fear. Spirituality would not be worth much if it did not acknowledge and embrace the full range of human experience at its very essence. After all, what makes an experience "uplifting" is not the absence of the darker emotions, but rather a complex mix of all that we bring to these moments. So much of what is powerful about spirituality (and psychotherapy also, for that matter) is that we are challenged to bring our light and our darkness together. If spirituality failed to welcome the darker, frightened or despairing side of our natures, it would only leave us feeling alienated.

Similarly, psychotherapists are not trying to bypass or "fix" human suffering. Instead, the goal is to validate and befriend ourselves and each other in times of suffering. The literature of spirituality is all about acknowledging that suffering is a necessary part of the human experience. We can recall the mythology of the hero's journey and remind ourselves that we are the heroes of our own journeys, including our various trials and failures. We still belong in our darker moments, maybe even more so, even though we may not always be in touch with that sense of belonging.

AWE

AWE AND THE CELEBRATION OF LIFE'S MYSTERY

The fairest thing we can experience is the mysterious. It is the fundamental emotion which stands at the cradle of true art and true science. He who knows it not and can no longer wonder, no longer feel amazement, is as good as dead, a snuffed-out candle.

—ALBERT EINSTEIN
The World As I See It

Awe is an intuition for the dignity of all things, a realization that things not only are what they are but also stand, however remotely, for something supreme. Awe is a sense for the transcendence, for the reference everywhere to mystery beyond all things.

—ABRAHAM JOSHUA HESCHEL
Who Is Man?

AWE AS FUNDAMENTAL

It seems right to begin with awe. "Awe" celebrates the mystery and wonder of life, but, unlike wonder, it can also include an element of fear or dread; it is reserved for that which is more powerful than we are or aspects of life that we can never fully know or understand. And because the feeling of awe must strike or grab us, we are not really in control of our experience. We cannot will ourselves to feel awe, although we can establish certain conditions or take on certain attitudes which are more conducive to strengthening the power of awe in our lives.

Most of us would probably agree with Einstein that there is something "fundamental" about recognizing the mysterious in life and being able to stand in wonder. Being in touch with mystery connects us with a sense of limitless possibility, both within ourselves as well as in the larger world. To experience awe is to feel momentarily liberated, a recognition that there is something magnificent that has the power to transcend our daily cares and concerns—but it is not just "out there," because we belong to it as well. We are part of it. When we feel awe we sense that we are operating from the place of our greatest wisdom and seeing ourselves and the world from the most enlightened and ultimately accurate perspective.

MYSTERY IS WHERE THE ACTION IS

Descartes concluded that the presence of infinity was the basis for the proof of the existence of God. Another interpretation is to see infinity as proof that life is far bigger and more complex than we can imagine and as proof that actual life does not fit into the neat boxes or categories that we create to try to explain it. Whether we believe in God or not, the existence of infinity suggests that mystery and the unknown or unknowable is woven into the fabric of life— that there is a kind of magic to it, and that life cannot be reduced or simplified in the ways that some of our traditional scientific thinking might imply.

In a sense, being in a state of awe is the opposite from believing in any specific doctrine or explanation of life. Awe is about the encounter with mystery and our inability to ever come to terms with the infinite. When we think of it this way, mystery does not represent a problem that we should try to solve or conquer. Quite the opposite: mystery is where the action is. And knowing this changes everything. Because mystery pervades all of life, from the infinite vastness of open space to the infinite complexity of an individual atom or cell, awe becomes a rational response to any aspect of life that we choose to examine, depending upon our ability to be open to it. As Abraham Joshua Heschel says, "Awe is a sense for the transcendence, for the reference everywhere to mystery beyond all things."

FINDING THE "MORE" IN THE MOMENT

Days pass and the years vanish, and we walk sightless among miracles.

—JEWISH PRAYER BOOK
Gates of Prayer

It is fair to say that most humans are guilty of walking "sightless among miracles." While we may have moments when we are struck with awe and experience the world around us in its true glory and infinite complexity, this is not our characteristic mode of being. It is easy for days to pass and years to vanish while we remain focused on our personal agendas and lose sight of the bigger picture and the mystery of this life that we are a part of.

Cultivating awe may require that we adopt a different vantage point. Awe is about the wonder that we experience when we stand still and observe reality closely enough to really take it in. Contemporary spirituality, mindfulness practices and experiential psychotherapy all encourage this kind of stillness; they help us to focus on and experience the richness of the present moment and the fullness of our possibilities as people. Much of what unites psychotherapy with contemporary spirituality is this emphasis on leaving room for awe by remaining receptive to what the present moment offers.

SPIRITUALITY AND THE PRESENT MOMENT

More than any of the other spiritual emotions, a contemporary spirituality is, at its essence, about awe—about using mindfulness meditation and other practices to help us to wake up from the sleep of unconsciousness and discover the possibilities that exist in the present moment. Just like psychotherapy, contemporary spirituality is about leading an examined as opposed to an unexamined life, but the emphasis is somewhat different. From the Buddhist perspective, the danger is that we remain lost in our ordinary level of consciousness and end up living like robots, as if in a dream from which we may never wake. When we are lost we are out of touch with ourselves and with the truth about who we are and what is out there in the world.

The problem, as many spiritual teachers might explain it, is that we lose touch with the mystery or magic of life because we resist being in the moment, in the "now." We fail to realize the basic truth that the present moment is all we have, that we will never be living anywhere but in the present. That is why mindfulness practices emphasize the "pause," the importance of consciously deciding to make the time to be in touch with whatever is real for us in the particular moment, no matter what type of moment it is. Without pausing, how can we take it all in, examine it and begin to appreciate or understand it?

Yet it is very human to resist doing this. So much of the time we experience a kind of restlessness or vague sense of dissatisfaction that we would just as soon run away from. Focusing on the past, thinking about the future, or taking actions to help move us forward in our lives usually feels more promising or productive. Particularly for young people who have most of their future ahead of them, the pressure to create the right future would appear to be a higher priority than lingering in present moments that are far from "awesome."

Our modern lifestyles contribute to the problem by offering the luxury and the curse of endless distractions that appear much more enticing than sitting on a meditation mat. But these pursuits can become counterproductive when we seek from them a level of gratification that they cannot ultimately provide, leaving us to assume that we just need more. Whether it is an updated kitchen with granite counter tops and stainless steel appliances, career success, a shopping spree, a better body, more money, more food, alcohol or drugs, the "highs" that these activities offer are often followed by "lows" if we are not finding other reliable sources of sustenance in our lives. As a culture, our quest for more may be better addressed by learning to find the "more" in the richness of the present moment.

THE ATTITUDES OF MINDFULNESS

So how do we go about finding this "more" and rekindling the sense of awe in our lives? The answer may be that what is needed is a type of spiritual practice where we redirect our attention and our attitudes so that we begin to experience our present moments differently. The mindfulness practice that we are most familiar with is meditation, where we are instructed to sit quietly for a certain amount of time each day and disengage our minds from the normal pursuit of thoughts. But mindfulness in the broader sense is not just about a meditation practice where we sit and let go of thoughts. It is also very much about self-observation and truly being in touch with where we are, and in order to do this, we need to adopt certain attitudes.

What is required is a willingness to look deeply at one's present moments, no matter what they hold, in a spirit of generosity, kindness toward oneself, and openness toward what might be possible.

—JON KABAT-ZINN
Wherever You Go, There You Are

Jon Kabat-Zinn, a Professor of Medicine Emeritus and founder of the Stress Reduction Clinic at the University of Massachusetts Medical School, is one of the leading figures in the world of contemporary spirituality, especially when it comes to teaching mindfulness practices and the attitudes that go with them. He emphasizes three key elements of a mindfulness attitude: the "willingness to look deeply" and honestly at what is actually there in a given moment; the importance of doing this in a spirit of "generosity" and "kindness toward oneself"; and the need to maintain an openness to what is possible.

We commit ourselves to taking on a different perspective—one that is focused and purposeful but, at the same time, allows us to be open and free of our usual judgments and expectations. While this takes some courage, it is also meant to be a heartfelt experience, not just a cold and analytic assessment. When we think about meditation we may not immediately associate it with an attitude of generosity or kindness, and yet this willingness to be kind to ourselves is an essential part of the practice.

WE ARE WELCOME AS WE ARE

Pema Chodron, another prominent voice in the world of contemporary spirituality, is an American Buddhist nun who is known for her fresh and often counterintuitive views, particularly when it comes to making room for the pain and suffering in our lives. Not surprisingly, she summarizes key features of a meditation practice in much the same way as Kabat-Zinn. As she describes in her book *Awakening Loving Kindness*, the path of meditation is about curiosity and inquisitiveness and involves three key attitudes: "being gentle, precise, and open." The challenge is to combine a spirit of good heartedness towards ourselves with a willingness to observe precisely what is there in the moment, "just as a scientist is not afraid to look into a microscope."

Of course it can feel a little scary to be asked to look closely and deeply at what is actually there in a given moment in our lives. We may be inclined to put off doing this until some future time when we imagine that the process might seem easier or more rewarding. But Chodron would disagree. She explains how people often tell her how they wanted to contact her earlier, but that they felt they should wait until they were more "together." And her response is to think, "Well, if you're anything like me, you could wait forever!" She encourages us to come as we are; this is where the magic lies.

Chodron makes it clear that meditation is not about trying to get rid of our egos or even trying to change or improve ourselves; in fact, the essence of the practice is just the opposite. She says it beautifully in her book *Comfortable With Uncertainty*: "Meditation practice isn't about trying to throw ourselves away and become something better. It's about befriending who we are already."

PARALLELS WITH PSYCHOTHERAPY

It is not a big leap to see parallels here with psychotherapy.

There is a great similarity between psychotherapy as it is practiced today and the approaches and attitudes described by Jon Kabat-Zinn and Pema Chodron. Just as mindfulness practices like meditation provide a structure for creating the opportunity to be quiet, listen and experience oneself in the universe without our endless mental activity, psychotherapy is a type of ritual we have devised which creates a structure for quieting our normal thought process and making the time and space to look honestly and precisely at our inner reality and to do so with kindness, respect and an openness to what we might discover.

You would not expect to see the word "awe" appearing frequently in psychoanalytic journals or academic books or articles assigned to students of psychology, yet the concept of awe has tremendous significance in the psychotherapy world. It is not so much that we establish a goal for our clients to experience more awe in their lives, although that would be a desirable outcome. The emphasis here is more on the need to make room for awe in the psychotherapy process.

As with contemporary spirituality, psychotherapists attempt to stay receptive to what the present moment offers. What is different is the way that we are receptive. In mediation we are encouraged to witness and let go of thoughts, feelings and sensations, while in experiential psychotherapy we are encouraged to express and explore them, but the focus of attention for both practices is on what is possible when we pause and let ourselves fully experience what is real in the moment.

THE MYSTERY OF OUR INNER LIVES

We are most accustomed to thinking of awe as a feeling that

we get when we glance up at the night sky and are reminded of the limitless universe beyond the world that we know, or when we ponder the mystery of the tiniest particles and how there appears to be no end to how small life can be. In psychotherapy we are dealing with a somewhat different dimension of the mysterious, but one that is equally worthy of inspiring awe—and that is the mystery of our inner lives and the infinite possibilities that our inner worlds offer. This same infinite more that we see in the night sky and in the smallest particle can be said to apply to our inner worlds as well. We are part of that mystery. The realm of who we are beneath the surface is infinitely intricate and never reaches an end.

Part of what we are doing as therapists is setting up the conditions to experience the moment with the client in its fullness, to help uncover the "more" within the client and in the moment between client and therapist, and finding that "more" helps the client move forward. It should not be surprising that the structure that we create and the attitudes we adopt in psychotherapy for bringing out the "more" within us are similar in some ways to spiritual practices for finding the "more," the awe, in any given moment. And of course there is no end, no limit, to what we can find and explore. We will never have enough time to fully fathom ourselves and to capture all that exists in our conscious and unconscious minds.

But the infinite aspect of our inner lives is not the only thing that should inspire awe. After all, we are not just receiving an endless number of random feelings and sensations from within ourselves. There is real meaning there as well. We know when something becomes meaningful to us. When we hear beautiful music or go to a museum or read poetry, we know when our full being is responding. And if we are writing or speaking with someone, we know when our communications carry real meaning and reflect something of importance to us that truly resonates. So much of what is awe-inspiring about psychotherapy is that we are establishing ideal conditions for clients to make contact with their inner worlds and to witness first hand these moments of meaning.

THE MIRACLE OF FELT MEANING

Rather than remaining within the paucity and unreliability of a theory, we employ all of them to open whole reaches of human experience.

—EUGENE GENDLIN
Focusing-Oriented Psychotherapy

WHAT MAKES PSYCHOTHERAPY WORK?

The experiential dimension of psychotherapy has been with us from the beginning, yet the process itself remains somewhat of a mystery. What exactly is this "more in the moment" that we are attempting to bring out in psychotherapy? Or, to ask a much more basic question, what makes psychotherapy work in the first place? And why do so many therapists today work in an experiential way, as opposed to emphasizing more structured or educational approaches?

Freud gave us one way to conceptualize the experiential process when he identified the realm of the unconscious and the possibility of "making the unconscious conscious." Today we are still very aware of the unconscious and the opportunities for uncovering unconscious material in psychotherapy, but most of us now think of experiential psychotherapy in a much broader way. We tend to think of it as a process where the client is able to connect with feelings—or, more specifically, a process where clients can check in with how they are feeling or feel about something and find words or images to express this. Connecting with feelings is now such a central feature of most psychotherapy that therapists are often parodied for always coming back to a client and asking, "How do you feel about that?"

But how do we define "feelings"? I prefer to use the word "touched." We might say that the goal of experiential psychotherapy is for the client to be touched in the process in a way that leads to growth and development. The advantage of the word "touched" is that it suggests something fresh and new, something that is felt in a palpable, bodily way and at the same time can encompass a wide range of experiences. It can mean emotionally touched (including the painful moments as well as the sweet or poignant ones); it can mean touched by the truth of a new insight; it can mean touched in the many ways that clients and therapists are touched in the psychotherapy relationship; and it can include a broader understanding of touching where a client can tap into an "underneath feeling level" below the surface of what is being said.

HOW WE ARE "TOUCHED" IN PSYCHOTHERAPY

For further clarification, I turn to the wok of Eugene Gendlin, an American philosopher and psychotherapist who has devoted much of his career to understanding what is happening in these moments when we feel touched in the psychotherapy process. Gendlin is also known as the founder of Focusing, a specific therapeutic approach that emerged from his collaboration with psychologist Carl Rogers. Gendlin has done psychotherapists a great service by giving us a very precise view of what the experiential dimension is all about. He would probably say that all of the forms of "touching" that I mentioned above are part of his vision of what promotes healing and growth in psychotherapy.

As a phenomenological philosopher, Gendlin is doing something quite different from most other psychologists or psychotherapists; rather than developing theoretical concepts about what is healing, Gendlin begins with concepts that describe the therapy process itself in its full intricacy and continuous movement and unfolding—what he calls "alive concepts." The use of alive concepts is a way of bringing the language of psychotherapy forward to better reflect the cutting edge of today's science and philosophy, including the new physics, complexity theory and postmodernism. Just as complexity theory describes the world in terms of systems nested within systems going out to infinity, alive concepts capture what is mysterious about the dynamic process of human experiencing.

Gendlin is also different from most psychoanalytic writers in his focus on "felt meaning" and its importance in psychotherapy. He began his philosophical inquiry as an attempt to better understand what he refers to as an "ah-ha moment"—that experience that most of us can relate to when we *sense* that something is right or meaningful. Felt meaning involves the body as well as the mind, not just the left brain, rational experience.

SPEAKING FROM A DEEPER PLACE

For Gendlin, the process of finding meaning is very much about our ability to connect with what he calls an "implicit" domain. Lynn Preston, Director of the Experiential Psychotherapy Project (EPP) in New York City, calls it a "flow of life process that is always present just beneath the content of what is being said." The implicit is similar to the unconscious in that we can be unaware of it when we are just functioning in a more superficial way. But unlike the unconscious, there is a fluidity in accessing the implicit realm; we have the ability to tap into it and speak from this infinitely intricate place within us. When we do, what comes out is totally unique, with its own kind of complexity—not something that could be entirely predicted in advance.

We as therapists depend upon this interplay between the implicit and the explicit for the therapy process to have momentum. After all, our clients are not just expressing what they already know but are allowing thoughts, feelings, images and reactions to emerge freshly out of their lived experience in the therapy process. Lynn Preston sums it up as follows: "A nutshell version of a focusing orientation is that it is a therapy centrally concerned with helping the client to speak from his feeling sense rather than about his feelings."

As Gendlin describes in his book *Focusing-Oriented Psychotherapy*, a specific sequence of events occurs when we experience moments of felt meaning. It begins with what he calls a "felt sense," which connects us with our deeper implicit realm. A felt sense "forms at the border zone between conscious and unconscious" (at the edge of awareness), comes to us in a visceral way and represents a whole complexity. Although a felt sense can include emotion, it is not the same thing as emotion. It is more like a whole bodily mood. When we tap in to the felt sense, emotion sometimes accompanies the process, but the felt sense also includes the bigger experience, the "place where the tears come from."

RECOGNIZING MOMENTS OF MEANING

When I was listened to for that mood—which has come to be called "a felt sense"—and invited to speak from it, I experienced a special kind of connection to myself and to a forward moving process. I found a direct line of access to the 'underneath feeling self'—the self that is sometimes hard to find, sometimes hard to bear and often hard to comprehend. I learned to touch into myself in this way and this self, amazingly came forward clearly speaking its own truths. New steps of awareness emerged organically, leading out to a hopeful, fresh, unexpected creativity.

—LYNN PRESTON
"Two Interwoven Miracles:
The Relational Dimension of Focusing-Oriented Psychotherapy"

As Lynn Preston describes, when someone finds just the right words to express their deeper felt sense, there is a feeling of connection, rightness and truth. Gendlin calls this the forward movement of a felt sense and believes that this is the basis of what works in psychotherapy. This is the moment of felt meaning. We know when we have found it because we can feel the shift, in the same way that we can feel the relief or release of an "ah-ha-moment." There is a sense of "emergence" when what had been implicit is made explicit.

Moments of emergence in therapy can be quite dramatic in a beautiful way, which is ironic since what is emerging or newly expressed by a client sometimes comes from hidden parts of themselves that may be associated with shame, vulnerability or fear. Clients may connect with sadness or other aspects of themselves that they normally would ignore or fail to express.

The client's words may be beautiful or hopeful ("Ah. . .so now I see what I have been missing all my life!") or they may be dark ("I realize now that I would rather be dead than alive.") But either way, if the client is speaking from a place of their emergent truth, it is safe to assume that the process will provide some type of forward movement. We want to encourage clients to say what has been "unsayable" in their lives, whether it is hopeful, dark or somewhere in between.

But emergence and forward movement are not just limited to dramatic moments. Much of the value of Gendlin's concepts is that they capture and explain a wide range of experiences, including those that are more subtle or that occur in small steps. In any given session, for example, there may be many times when a thought or a word or an image comes to a client in a way that feels meaningful, or when we feel touched in some way in the psychotherapy relationship. We might think of psychotherapy as the sum of these kinds of moments, both large and small, that feel right to us and offer us a sense of direction as to how to proceed—both in the psychotherapy process as well as in our lives in general.

FACILITATING EMERGENCE

To a large extent, the role of the therapist has shifted from one who holds the answers or the truth to one who facilitates a dialogue that leads to forward movement. As a therapist, I like to think of my goal as "facilitating emergence." One way to do this is to encourage clients to slow down and check in with what they are experiencing in the present moment rather than staying caught at the more superficial, conversational level. As with contemporary spirituality, we want to "honor the pause" and resist the temptation to rush in to fill up quiet times; we want to avoid sending the message that we are in a hurry or that we are more concerned with analyzing or educating than with experiencing.

This does not mean, however, that the therapist is passive or just sits back and waits for something to emerge. Felt meaning does not take place in a vacuum; what emerges for a client is very much influenced by their relationship to and interactions with the therapist. So, in addition to leaving room for the client to make contact with their inner experience, facilitating emergence is also very much about the way that the therapist listens and responds to what is being said.

As Lynn Preston is fond of saying, therapists need to be "evocateurs." We want to listen with an appreciation for what might emerge, which involves our own felt sensing, our ability to sense the "more" of what the client is wanting to express. We want to interact with our clients in a way to help evoke the felt sense level, lift it out, welcome it, explore it, cultivate it, mark it and celebrate it (although these steps are not necessarily done with words). This is a far cry from the old psychoanalytic stance of neutrality, where the emphasis was placed on interpretation (of transference, etc.) rather than on forward movement through the emergence of felt meaning.

THE DANCE BETWEEN THERAPIST AND CLIENT

It follows that facilitating emergence is not something that the therapist undertakes as a removed, objective observer. At any given moment both the therapist and the client are impacting each other in infinitely complex ways. As two human beings engaged in a process of discovery, the therapist and the client are both intricately involved in their own felt sensing. It is difficult to help our clients tap into deeper levels if we are not also doing this ourselves. As evocateurs we use our felt sensing along with our rational, left brain thinking to help us guide the therapy process.

This happens in a variety of ways. Even when we are just listening we use our own felt sense to get a feeling for the often elusive "more in the moment" that the client is wanting to express. But so much of what we do goes beyond listening skills. Emergence also occurs through spontaneous conversation or improvisation, where the therapist assumes a more active role. According to Preston, "The therapeutic process is often an interplay of the slowing down and sensing into of focusing, and the spontaneous back and forth of conversation." As therapists, we want to be skilled at the creative use of ourselves, which involves a kind of "coming from underneath," an ability to access and act upon our own felt sense in a more spontaneous way. As Preston puts it:

> *The therapist is like a dance partner in the twists and turns of implicit emergence. It's something that the two people are doing together, not only that one person is helping the other to do. Although the roles are different, both partners are equally struggling to be present, coordinated with each other, to find their way together toward a future that is centered in the present moment.*

THE THERAPIST'S PARADOX

Of course our role as therapists is not limited to being evocateurs. Clients also need us to offer feedback and suggestions, educate them and provide a certain amount of structure. Yet having a sense of purpose in this way requires concentration and limits (to some degree) our ability to be open and receptive. I call this "the therapist's paradox." Learning to juggle the proactive, willful, more conceptual aspect of our jobs with what might be called a more "spiritual," open approach can be a wonderful although challenging journey.

When I was first introduced to Gendlin's concepts, I assumed that his approach would be strictly "client-centered" in the tradition of Carl Rogers, with an emphasis on a receptive stance that encourages a client to find their own way and leaves plenty of room for the emergence of felt meaning. As such, I imagined that his focusing-oriented style would be incompatible with other types of therapy that demand a more pro-active stance, such as cognitive therapy, guided imagery, EMDR, stress reduction work, behavioral therapy, etc. I had the impression that therapists needed to choose between these seemingly incompatible styles.

When I studied Gendlin's philosophy I was surprised and much relieved to find that he did not disapprove of more proactive types of therapy and, in fact, he advocated using a wide range of psychotherapy approaches. He described how a focusing orientation could be used in conjunction with other theories, concepts and approaches to provide the right balance. This is true because theories and concepts are more like "things" while focusing is more about how we make use of the potential for aliveness and forward movement in each moment, in the "now."

We can always ask ourselves if our interventions are helping the client to tap into a deeper implicit level and if they are contributing to forward movement. Our theories, concepts and agendas can be seen merely as hypotheses to be discarded if they do not contribute to the emergence of felt meaning.

No matter how strongly we are attached to any particular concept or approach, we need this discipline if we are to make room for "awe" and that unpredictable "more" in the moment.

THE SPIRITUAL DIMENSION OF FELT MEANING

Meaning must be constantly received, like the light to which
we must open our eyes here and now, if we want to see.
—BROTHER DAVID STEINDL-RAST
"Word, Silence, and Understanding"

TWO PERSPECTIVES ON FELT MEANING

Although they come from very different backgrounds, I have noticed some striking similarities between Eugene Gendlin's philosophy and the writings of Brother David Steindl-Rast. Gendlin is not considered a spiritual writer, and Brother David is a Benedictine monk and is not a psychotherapist. But what they are focusing on and the way they think lead them to come to similar conclusions, although they use different language. In a sense, both are phenomenological philosophers in that both are closely documenting a person's inner process of experiencing. And both could be called spiritual in that they are asking the big questions, such as what creates aliveness and how it is that we find meaning in our lives.

The parallels between the two are probably possible because of Brother David's basic orientation. In addition to being a Benedictine monk, he has also studied Zen Buddhism and has received the Martin Buber Award for his achievements in building bridges between the East and the West. He is a unique spiritual leader, someone who has been described as a contemplative or a mystic but who also is highly credible in the academic world (and held a prestigious lectureship at Cornell University following the likes of Paul Tillich).

Like Gendlin, Brother David never loses sight of the infinite and the mysterious. In fact, Brother David's definition of spirituality is based on the notion of mystery; he believes that Mystery (he uses a capital "M") is not a problem to be resolved but rather is something to be embraced. This is the territory of the infinite and what he calls the "More." In his article "Views of the Cosmos," he claims that "the encounter with Mystery is our basic religious experience." This is the way we confront "a power beyond our comprehension," and to do so means that we must have an open view of the world that acknowledges and incorporates Mystery.

FINDING MEANING AS AN ONGOING PROCESS

One reason that Brother David's writings are particularly relevant to psychotherapy is that he is interested in the human quest for meaning, but not just in the narrow sense of looking for an explanation of where we came from or for the answers to the mysteries of the universe. Rather, he is focused on how we find meaning on an ongoing basis in our lives. He explains that finding meaning is a process, not something that, once found, one can hold onto and claim to possess; we cannot expect to keep meaning once we find it. Instead, "Meaning must be constantly received, like the light to which we must open our eyes here and now, if we want to see."

Because experiential psychotherapy is all about creating moments of felt meaning and forward movement, it may not be surprising that Brother David's writings about finding meaning are similar in many ways to Gendlin's. As in Gendlin's philosophy, we always come back to the "now" and the fresh possibilities for felt meaning inherent in each moment. And like Gendlin, Brother David emphasizes that the experience of finding meaning is not something that we can will to happen. Unlike purpose, finding meaning is not subject to our control. This kind of meaning is more about letting go or allowing than it is about willing. As Gendlin might say, felt meaning emerges; it has a life of its own.

FINDING MEANING CAN BE AN ADVENTURE

When a client experiences felt meaning and forward movement in psychotherapy, should we consider this a spiritual process? Most of us would probably not think of this as spiritual, yet Brother David's language adds a spiritual dimension in that he highlights the uplifting elements of the human quest for meaning—something that we might be tempted to take for granted. For Brother David, there is no doubt that meaning is connected to spirituality. He tells us in "Word, Silence, and Understanding" that "happiness and meaningful life are inseparable" and that spirituality is "no more and no less than meaningful living, religion realized in daily life."

> *As long as I am in control, not much can happen to me. As soon as I allow reality to "touch me," I am in for adventure. The quest for meaning is the adventure par excellence, and happiness lies in the thrill of this adventure.*
> —BROTHER DAVID STEINDL-RAST
> "Word, Silence, and Understanding"

31

Brother David reminds us how exciting the quest for meaning is, that it can be thrilling to take the risk of really allowing reality to touch us. And of course psychotherapy is an ideal structure for clients to learn to take that risk and to participate in the experience of felt meaning. We encourage clients to relinquish some of their normal control and undertake this adventure. This aspect of psychotherapy is the source of much of its power and a primary reason that clients are willing to come back week after week. And at the same time, the need to let go of some of their control is also the reason why many people who might benefit from and enjoy psychotherapy manage to avoid embarking on the adventure.

Hearing the client's story in psychotherapy is not just about the content that is revealed or what we learn as a result, although this is vitally important. It is also about participating in the process of finding meaning, and the happiness and satisfaction that comes from that process. When we invite clients to open up and tell their story, we tend to think of the benefits in a traditional way—that the client will get to know themselves better and that doing this in the presence of an accepting therapist will help them overcome any negative self-concept. And also that, with the help of the therapist, clients will become more aware of and learn to correct counterproductive patterns that have been holding them back. But to this list we should add that the process of finding meaning on an ongoing basis in psychotherapy is healing and fulfilling in and of itself and can establish a precedent for the adventure Brother David is referring to.

THE COMPONENTS OF FELT MEANING

My first question when I read Brother David's thoughts on meaning was whether he was really referring to the same type of felt meaning that clients experience in psychotherapy. Is meaning by Brother David's definition the same as what Gendlin describes, where the client taps into an "underneath feeling self," finds the right words or image, and experiences a shift or a sense of forward movement? To my surprise, I discovered that the way Brother David breaks down the components of felt meaning is remarkably similar to Gendlin's description.

Brother David believes that what makes life meaningful differs from person to person, but when something becomes meaningful it always includes three aspects: silence ("the mysterious matrix from which word emerges"), word (where word can be defined broadly to include "whatever carries meaning"), and understanding. He explains that if we can allow ourselves to sink deeply into the silence, it can express itself in words, and then we have understanding. This sounds remarkably like Gendlin, where silence represents the implicit realm, "word" represents the words or images that express the felt sense, and understanding represents the felt shift and forward movement.

FELT MEANING AND THE HEART

I find some of Brother David's language particularly beautiful and, as a result, it is easy for me to relate to as I go about my work as a therapist. For Brother David, meaning is something that nourishes us. In "The God Problem," he describes meaning as "some encounter or activity in which your heart finds rest—for a while at least." I love that he brings in the concept of the heart when he talks about meaning. When our bodies respond in those "ah-ha" moments, it makes sense that our hearts are also involved; they go from a place of restlessness to finding rest. This is

Brother David's way of describing that sense of release or relief characteristic of meaningful moments.

I also appreciate that both Gendlin and Brother David are fascinated with this mysterious place of silence that we all have within us and the fact that it contains more than can ever be expressed. Gendlin calls it the "implicit" realm and uses the term "implicit intricacy" to convey this infinitely complex quality. These words bring to mind the infinite fullness at the depths of our being and our longing to bring this into the world. The fact that the silent place includes the heart makes sense, since so much of the fullness feels like love.

Ultimately love and finding meaning belong together. This is an important concept for therapists. Being reminded of the fullness of our place of silence and the possibilities for the "more" within each of us can help us during those difficult or not so meaningful times in therapy. Therapists can remember that this mysterious place of silence is always there in its potential fullness, and if we remain patient we may be surprised by what emerges.

MEANINGFUL DIALOGUE

Another feature of Brother David's exploration of felt meaning is that he does not focus solely on the individual; he also addresses the issue of how people find meaning together when they are in conversation. Of course not every conversation in our lives needs to feel meaningful. Nothing is wrong with a certain amount of "chatter," even in psychotherapy. It would be exhausting and annoying to feel that we must always be accessing and speaking from our deeper places of silence. Yet clearly the challenge in psychotherapy is to leave enough room amidst the chatter to find the more meaningful moments.

Brother David offers a definition of "real dialogue" that is particularly useful for psychotherapists. For Brother David, "real dialogue" is not just an exchange of words but rather "an exchange of silence with silence by means of words." He explains that when we are in real dialogue (in any type of interaction), we go "deep down into the silent part of the other." So even though we think of therapy as focusing on meaning from the standpoint of the client, real dialogue by this definition requires that both people be in contact with their own and each-others place of silence. Unless therapist and client can go "deep down into the silent part of the other," how can the client and therapist really be attuned?

If we believe that psychotherapy should meet Brother David's definition of real dialogue, we as therapists must be in contact with our own deep place of silence; we can't just help the client to connect to their place of silence while we remain detached. And we must also be willing to have the client witness our process to some degree. We might choose to speak directly to them from our place of silence, or, as often happens, the client simply experiences a connection with our place of silence without our needing to use words. I am not suggesting here that we as therapists should give up our boundaries and become overly self-disclosing, but rather that we must maintain our disciplined roles while at the same time skillfully accessing our own felt sensing, whether we are listening, responding or being more creative or spontaneous.

EXAMPLES OF FELT MEANING

What follows are two simple examples from psychotherapy

that illustrate this process of finding meaning. First, I will cite a case where the words of my client served to connect us to the silent place of each other. This was my first session with a young male client who was coming to therapy for the first time and acknowledging how much pain he had been in for much of his life. He conveyed a combination of sadness, anger, frustration and fear. Toward the end of the session he grew quiet for a moment and then said with some emotion, "I am an ugly person." It was clear to me in that moment that there was something of great value in his making this statement. I felt touched, and in the pause that followed I experienced a feeling of connection—and I knew he could tell that I was moved.

It is still not totally clear to me all that was conveyed by his sentence, but I felt that he did not need me to reassure him that he was not an ugly person. (I later found out that his parents had been reassuring him all his life about what a sweet, attractive and good person he is.) In that moment he needed to say this unsayable thing to me and have me receive it at a deep level as the gift that it was. Without my putting it into words, in that moment we were both able to connect with the deep, silent part of the other.

The second example illustrates an instance where I spoke from my own place of silence to help facilitate a meaningful dialogue. A client is speaking of an unpleasant dream about a former friend with whom she is now estranged, and as I look at her face I sense that something is troubling her as she speaks. I use my felt sense and without giving it much thought, I share with her that I have had recurring dreams as well about a friend who I am estranged from. (The reason I chose to go in this direction was that I sensed that her concern was coming from a negative judgment about herself, that being estranged from this friend suggested some defect in herself.) I then told my client, "Yes, dreams like that can have a haunting quality." I emphasized the word "haunting," which to me captured so much of the rawness and complexity of what was troubling about my own experience with a failed friendship. To my delight, she brightened up and responded, "Yes, it does have a haunting feeling!"

This is an example where just one word served to connect the two of us in our deep places of silence and provided a special kind of forward movement. I believe that my client was reassured that she was not alone or abnormal, and the word "haunting" convinced her that I indeed had experienced something very similar to what she was going through—this word conveyed in a fresh, new way some of the disturbing quality of both of our experiences. In the course of our exchange we each felt deeply understood and appreciated.

CONCLUSIONS: FELT MEANING AND PSYCHOTHERAPY

As a field that once aspired to be a science, it has been difficult for our profession to openly acknowledge and celebrate the wondrous aspects of what we do. I believe that the language of felt meaning gives us one way to do this; it describes processes that are so central to what actually happens in psychotherapy and yet have not previously been made explicit. This language can inspire us and remind us of the "miracle" that occurs when we experience felt meaning and a sense of forward movement in psychotherapy or in any other facet of our lives.

Hearing these words strengthens our own felt sensing ability in the same way that regular exercise strengthens our muscles or going to church or to spiritual retreats can open us up to awe and the possibilities that each moment holds. In our role as "evocateurs" we need the exposure to the evocative language to help us embody the kind of "aliveness" that might be called spiritual.

HELP WITH ORIENTATION

The language of felt meaning also offers a valuable perspective from which to view our work as therapists, an occupation in which it is easy to sometimes feel lost, even after many years of study and experience. For me, what sticks in my mind most are certain phrases that help to ground me and remind me of my priorities. I like to remember that my primary role is to "facilitate emergence" and that I can navigate using my own felt sense to help uncover the "more" of what wants to be said and to lift out and celebrate "moments of meaning."

To appreciate that the heart responds when something becomes meaningful—that is a radical concept, though somewhat obvious when you think about it. The heart is not just reserved for the strictly interpersonal dimension of the psychotherapy relationship. We also very much use our hearts to sense where the "more" lies and to find meaning for the client and ourselves in the process. The right words can touch us in our place of deep silence and bring us to understanding, which we can recognize as a felt shift or a place where our hearts find rest.

THE THERAPIST'S PARADOX

The presence of paradox may be one way to recognize when we are in the realm of the spiritual, the awe-inspiring, when we are experiencing life in its full complexity. As therapists, we come face to face with paradox in many different forms. Just the basic premise that we are helping people to grow and change by accepting and embracing where they are right now is paradoxical.

One aspect of our role that is not often discussed is the paradoxical position that we are placed in of needing to be purposeful and receptive at the same time. If we as therapists are to remain open to the emergence of felt meaning, we must hold the tension between these two seemingly contradictory states. I was heartened to discover that both Gendlin and Brother David consider this tension to be legitimate. Just like a monk who learns to remain fully present while doing everyday chores such as washing dishes, we as therapists can practice staying fully present with our clients even as we are purposefully guiding the psychotherapy process.

Therapists need not feel wrong or guilty about using cognitive therapy or other more proactive approaches in their practices. Quite the opposite: the willingness to rise to the challenge and commit to both purpose and openness to meaning is a source of strength and something that can benefit our clients. We can proudly embrace both the purposeful and the receptive aspects of our work.

RETURNING TO AWE

As noted earlier, because mystery pervades all of life, awe becomes a rational response to any aspect of life that we choose to examine, depending upon our ability to be open to it. Yet we may be more likely to feel awe when we observe a colorful sunset, a hummingbird or a rose than when we contemplate "the Mystery at the center of our own heart." Maybe because the mystery within us is not something that we can see, we are less likely to experience it as awesome or beautiful.

We discover Mystery at the center of our own heart and sense the staggering possibility that our own little life may become ultimately meaningful as a celebration of that Mystery in which it is rooted.
—BROTHER DAVID STEINDL-RAST
"Views of the Cosmos"

Brother David's words help us to recognize this beauty—"the staggering possibility that our own little life may become ultimately meaningful as a celebration of that Mystery in which it is rooted." What a delightful way to celebrate who we are, not in an ego centric way, but as a part of that larger mystery in which we are rooted. As Heschel says, "Awe is an intuition for the dignity of all things, a realization that things not only are what they are but also stand, however remotely, for something supreme." Certainly our "own little life" deserves to be included too, as standing, however remotely, for something supreme.

IS PSYCHOTHERAPY A SPIRITUAL PRACTICE?

I have often felt that therapists are engaging in a kind of spiritual practice. Part of it, I believe, is that we are assuming the same attitudes that Jon Kabat-Zinn and Pema Chodron outline as the essential features of a mindfulness approach: together with our clients we are examining the present moment with precision in a spirit of kindness and openness to all that is possible. And in doing so we create a sacred space for our clients that is not so much a reflection of our individual personalities but more a reflection of the special role that we have taken on.

But much of what feels spiritual about psychotherapy *is* about our individual personalities and who we are as people. We are in an occupation that allows us to regularly witness and experience the miracle of felt meaning and the feelings of connection to our clients (and to ourselves) that come with sharing these moments. We learn over time that the experience of felt meaning is not just passive. We have the opportunity to open our hearts to all that is happening at the experiential level, both for ourselves and for our clients. As therapists we make this gesture when we actively recognize, evoke and celebrate moments of meaning.

Brother David describes "the quest for meaning" as "the adventure par excellence"—that willingness to give up control enough to allow reality to touch us. Other than extreme sports, where we take risks and give up some of our control in a physical way, it is difficult to imagine any endeavor in life that is more actively committed to this type of adventure than psychotherapy. The whole purpose of experiential psychotherapy is for the client to feel touched in a way that leads to healing and development. Ideally the quest for meaning that we undertake in psychotherapy provides a precedent for a lifetime of adventure, long after the actual psychotherapy is over and the client and therapist have parted ways.

FAITH

WHAT IS FAITH?

An act of faith is an act of a finite being who is grasped by and turned to the infinite.

—PAUL TILLICH
Dynamics of Faith

I would like to explore the experiential dimension of faith. Ultimately I want to examine faith and its counterpart, doubt, from the point of view of the psychotherapist. But before doing this I will step back and ask the more basic question: How can we define faith in a way that applies to a wide range of people, including those who consider themselves "spiritual but not religious"?

When we consider faith as one of the spiritual emotions it takes on an entirely different meaning than when it is used to designate a particular type of religious belief. If we asked someone to describe their faith, for example, we would expect to hear an answer such as Presbyterian or Catholic or Unitarian or Agnostic. But if we ask someone if they have faith, the answer is likely to be much more nuanced and complex. Having faith in a general sense suggests a trust in life, a source of comfort or ease. We might say that we have faith, even if we do not believe in a personal God who is watching over us and hears our prayers, or a heaven that awaits us after we die.

Faith is too broad a concept to confine to religion, and yet to call it "spiritual" implies more than just trust in the most basic sense. We might trust that we will wake up in the morning and that the day will proceed without any unexpected horrors, and this is truly a blessing for those of us who are fortunate enough to possess this basic trust. But the word "faith" in the context of a discussion of spirituality suggests something more, something we have faith in that is beyond the ordinary and the mundane.

FAITH AS A RELATIONSHIP WITH THE INFINITE

I propose that we think of faith as Paul Tillich described it: "An act of faith is an act of a finite being who is grasped by and turned to the infinite." The beauty of this description is that it is quite specific and yet is independent of the content of our faith; it could be said to include anyone who has a particular type of relationship with the infinite, whether they call themselves religious, spiritual, or anything else.

And he is not just speaking of a basic trust in life but is focusing on all that is implied by the word "infinite." The infinite stands for the transcendent, that quality of life that defies our normal boundaries or explanations and that encompasses the mysterious. The infinite symbolizes the extra-ordinary—the ultimate reality that escapes our rational understanding.

For Tillich, having a relationship with the infinite goes well beyond simply contemplating the endless expanse of the universe. Faith is not just about our thoughts or the conclusions that we have drawn about ultimate reality, nor is it just a process of willing to believe. His definition of faith includes a cognitive element and a behavioral element, since he speaks of an "act" where we are "turned to" the infinite;

but it also includes an emotional or "ecstatic" element, in that we must be "grasped by" the infinite. Faith includes all of these elements, the unconscious as well as the conscious, the ego, the superego, the cognitive and the emotional.

Brother David Steindl-Rast makes a similar point in "The Monk in Us" when he discusses the relationship between faith and truth. Faith is not just an intellectual process where we settle on some truth and hold onto it. Faith is really the opposite. It is about our ability to fully open ourselves and to experience what is true for us in a more visceral way. Rather than hold truth, truth is something "that holds us." He claims that "faith is precisely the letting go and letting truth hold us."

FAITH AND DOUBT GO TOGETHER

We tend to think of faith and doubt as opposites, but if we examine these concepts in more detail it becomes clear why this is not the case. If we lived in a world of certainty, without mystery or the challenge of infinity, then why would we need faith? If we fully understood the origins and nature of the universe and had the answers to all of our questions about the purpose and meaning of life, then the word "faith" would not need to exist. It would not be necessary to take the "leap of faith" because the nature of ultimate reality would be a certainty to us.

The concept of faith is only relevant in an uncertain world which, by definition, defies rational explanation. But the lack of certainty also invites doubt, just as it offers the opportunity for faith. Faith and doubt are like two sides of the same coin. There is an aspect of faith that feels certain in that there is an experience of the sacred. This is the aspect of faith that grasps us or holds us. But as finite beings attempting to come to terms with the infinite, the element of uncertainty is also present.

Doubt is not the opposite of faith; it is an element of faith.
—PAUL TILLICH
Systematic Theology, Volume 2

Tillich explains that faith must always include some form of separation from the object of faith. After all, if we do not experience any separation from the object of our faith—if we are able to know it fully and experience it consistently—then our experience would be one of certainty, which is not the same thing as faith. Separation goes hand and hand with the experience of faith. For most of us at least, we are not always in touch with our feelings of faith. Faith is not something that we can expect to access on a consistent basis.

When considered in this way, faith is not in conflict with reason; instead, it offers an alternative way to respond to the mysterious aspects of life. Faith allows us to approach the dimension of life that is unfathomable—something that reason alone cannot do.

MYTHS AS SYMBOLS

Because of this inherent uncertainty, Tillich claims that ultimate reality can only be described symbolically. We develop what he calls "myths." When our myths are seen as symbols rather than taken literally as truths, this represents a "dynamic" type of faith that allows for doubt and uncertainty. In contrast, "non-dynamic" faith excludes the possibility of uncertainty. When myths or symbols are taken literally as the ultimate truth, this does not represent the kind of "dynamic faith" that Tillich is describing.

This may explain why Tillich is considered somewhat controversial in certain circles and why his views have been rejected by some who are religious in a more traditional sense. But the fact that he examines faith from the broadest perspective, independent of the specific content of faith, makes his ideas particularly relevant to a discussion of contemporary spirituality. And the way that he introduces doubt as a necessary complement to faith offers a helpful reminder to all of us, including psychotherapists, that both faith and doubt have legitimate roles to play. We need to include both if we are to understand how the therapist experiences faith and the lack of faith as we navigate with the client through the psychotherapy hour.

THE 23RD PSALM AS METAPHOR

If faith is not defined as a commitment to a personal God or to a belief system about the origins or purpose of the universe, does it even make sense to use the term "faith"? I believe that it does make sense to use the term "faith" for people who are spiritually-oriented, even though their experience of faith may not be associated with any specific belief system. In order to understand a spiritual type of faith, we must look at the actual experience that we associate with spirituality, even though that presents certain challenges. Rather than ask what a spiritual person has faith in, we can ask what faith actually feels like to someone with a spiritual orientation.

I suggest that we look at it more as a faith in life itself and a faith that stems from an ongoing relationship to those aspects of life that embody the infinite quality that Tillich refers to. I understand that this view is ultimately subjective and may not resonate for everyone who considers themselves to be on a spiritual path.

A "SPIRITUAL" VIEW OF THE 23RD PSALM

I propose to look at the 23rd Psalm through the eyes of someone who is spiritual but not necessarily religious. This psalm offers a poetic description of the lifetime journey of faith that I believe captures the essence of certain aspects of faith better than any philosophical or theoretical descriptions.

And by interpreting the 23rd Psalm as a metaphor rather than literally, it provides a basis for understanding faith in a broader, spiritual way—a faith in those qualities of life that offer peace and fulfillment, and when fully recognized, allow us to guide our lives so as to reinforce these positive experiences.

The Lord is my shepherd; I shall not want.
He maketh me to lie down in green pastures: he leadeth
me beside the still waters.
He restoreth my soul: he leadeth me in the paths of
righteousness for his name's sake.
Yea, though I walk through the valley of the shadow of
death, I will fear no evil: for thou art with me; thy rod
and thy staff they comfort me.
Thou preparest a table before me in the presence of mine
enemies: thou annointest my head with oil; my cup
runneth over.
Surely goodness and mercy shall follow me all the days of
my life: and I will dwell in the house of the Lord forever.

In the years of reciting the 23rd Psalm in my youth, I had always considered it a chore and never was much interested in what it was saying. Now that I am older, the psalm has great meaning for me—in particular the phrase "as I walk through the valley of the shadow of death." As we get closer to the end of our walk through the valley, and as "the shadow of death" looms larger and begins to feel very real, the concepts of faith conveyed in this psalm become particularly relevant and compelling.

So much of what is captivating about the 23rd Psalm is that it is not describing a world of safety, but rather one that is fraught with evil, enemies, and potential danger. It is about the power of faith in a world of certain death and in the face of the many other challenges and difficulties that we encounter along the way.

THE ABILITY TO RESTORE OUR SOULS

The 23rd Psalm points out that there is a right way to live. There is an answer that life itself provides. One might say that there is an experience of being alive at a deep level that is restorative. We don't have to wait for an afterlife in order to reap our rewards; there are "green pastures" that we can lie down in, "still waters" that we can walk besides, and a "path of righteousness" that we can follow. We need not fear evil and we need not "want." Instead of fear, emptiness or deprivation, we can experience peace and fulfillment, a place where our needs are more than met, where our cup "runneth over," suggesting even the possibility of joy.

The 23rd Psalm is not simply referring to what makes us happy, but rather to something much more profound. It refers to what "restores our souls." Unlike a shopping spree, professional success, winning the lottery or other more worldly sources of happiness, finding that which truly restores our souls may demand much more of us. We may first need to conquer some of our own demons along the way; we must be capable of finding, taking in, and appreciating those green pastures and still waters that are truly restorative. Being on a spiritual path begins with recognizing how life can restore our souls and what the path of righteousness means for us.

FAITH TO GUIDE US THROUGH THE VALLEY

In the 23rd Psalm, "the Lord" is the shepherd, the source of all knowledge, the one who leads, who knows the way, who guides us through the valley, comforts us and protects us from our enemies. If we are to look at it metaphorically, the Lord could represent our own faith and wisdom, the part of ourselves that knows at the deepest level where the green pastures and still waters are, the part of ourselves that is strong, that we can count on to protect us and that will help keep us pointed in the right direction, on the path of righteousness.

My response to this is that it feels right that I can be my own shepherd, but only to the extent that I can experience a connection or alignment with what I would call a larger dimension of goodness or wisdom—something beyond myself. Yet I am unable to draw any conclusions as to what that means; I know that I feel connected to and aligned with some bigger "something," yet it is not a "thing." By being in touch with this source of wisdom, I can feel guided and comforted.

This is the aspect of faith that we are "grasped by." It is the emotional component, the experience of the sacred that gives us a sense of certainty along with the doubts that also accompany faith. Yet the term "grasped" should not be taken to imply that we are overtaken by faith in one ecstatic moment, like the Buddha who discovered the key to enlightenment while sitting under the Bodhi tree.

For most of us, the process of developing our spirituality or finding our way on our spiritual paths is likely to be much more subtle, a process that evolves over years or, more likely, decades. Often in spite of ourselves we finally learn to turn away from sources of gratification, excitement or comfort that ultimately fail to nourish us, and increasingly we look for a different kind of gratification, hopefully the kind that places us on our own particular version of the path of righteousness.

PRIORITIZING FAITH

As Tillich said, faith encompasses all the aspects of the personality, including the cognitive and the behavioral along with the emotional and the experiential. We must have knowledge about the route to take through the valley; we must have learned from our experiences and have translated that into a map of how to best proceed. This requires some sort of an intellectual commitment, even if we have not fully articulated it, to a certain kind of journey and certain ways of living. We sense that our maps are there, even if they are vague much of the time or, as can be expected, we fail to follow them consistently.

And there is also the behavioral element, the "tuning towards" that Tillich describes. Faith is about our journey. We don't necessarily start with a great deal of faith, but our faith can be reinforced when we turn towards and prioritize those behaviors and life experiences that are truly rewarding and nurturing.

Of course, our commitment to our path of righteousness may not always win over other commitments or other temptations that move us in opposing directions. But we can always return to our sources of wisdom for guidance. The more we are turned towards these aspects of life, the more we renew and validate our faith, leading to what I call the virtuous cycle of faith. Faith is something that we must first experience, but also recognize, believe in, nurture and prioritize in our lives.

DWELLING IN THE HOUSE OF THE LORD

But what about the peace that would come from believing that we will dwell in the house of the Lord forever? The 23rd Psalm offers the vision not only of an existence where goodness and mercy will follow us all of the days of our lives, but also that we will find our place with the Lord after we die. If we look at the 23rd Psalm as a metaphor rather than as a literal statement about the promise of safety or of the existence of a heaven, the question then becomes, "What does dwelling in the house of the Lord symbolize?"

Interestingly, the 23rd Psalm does not specifically state that goodness and mercy will always follow us or that a heaven necessarily awaits us. Rather, it is describing the feeling of its narrator, that as one who has been led by the shepherd Lord, it seems only natural to conclude that, "surely, goodness and mercy will follow me" and that "I will dwell in the house of the Lord forever." The word "surely" is key, since the narrator is acknowledging that there is no guarantee as to our safety in life or our status after our death, but that it feels right to conclude that we will ultimately be safe and protected.

A symbolic rather than a literal interpretation of the 23rd Psalm might emphasize these feelings of safety and protection that we experience on a spiritual path. We do not have to believe in a literal heaven or redemption or an afterlife for this psalm to deeply resonate. If we know fulfillment in the present moment, if we can truly say, "my cup runneth over," then that can be enough to give us a sense of peace about the future, whether in life or in death. What matters most is not whether we know the course that our future takes or what actually happens after we die; what is most relevant is how we feel about it and the peace that we experience in the present as a result.

When we are following our faith, when our souls feel restored, we need not focus on the past or fear the possibility of future pain or suffering. The experience of faith, grace, belonging or whatever you wish to call it, is so complete that it is somehow timeless. Faith in this sense is built upon something that we "know" in the present moment, rather than on a specific belief in redemption or a guarantee of life after death. In these moments of restoration, when our cups runneth over, the perfection and fullness of the present moment feels complete and the "now" feels eternal, as if we will dwell in the house of the Lord forever.

WHY WE ARE NOT ALONE

"Together" is the word that marks the goal of the religious quest.
—BROTHER DAVID STEINDL-RAST
Gratefulness, the Heart of Prayer

Even with the virtuous cycle of faith and the opportunity to guide our lives in directions that help restore our souls, are we not still alone? How can this spiritual faith compare to a more traditional religious faith where a personal God knows and understands us and has the power to intervene on our behalf? With a traditional religious orientation we entertain the possibility of a real relationship with God. But if God is simply a symbol for the wonder and mystery of life, where does that leave us? What is our relationship and how do we connect?

The key to the spiritual type of faith is that it does offer us a way to connect. At its essence, spirituality is about an ongoing relationship that we have with ultimate reality, or with the "infinite" as Tillich describes it. Part of the challenge of understanding spiritual faith is that this relationship with the infinite is difficult to describe and may not look the same from one person to the next.

In my experience, my earlier efforts to understand spirituality left me with certain phrases and concepts, but these words did not give me a sense of what my relationship with the infinite would actually feel like. I knew that spirituality was about unity and that we should somehow feel at one with the universe, and that our small ego self was often to blame for interfering with our ability to see the world as it truly is or to experience our own true selves—"who we really are." Part of the problem that I had with these explanations is that they seemed to focus on the negative, with the implication that we must get rid of (or dampen down) our ego selves in order to see clearly.

I offer here several definitions of spirituality that may help bring to life how we actually experience a relationship with the infinite. I have looked to three leading figures in the world of religion or spirituality to see how they have attempted to define what spirituality is. No doubt there are many different definitions of spirituality out there, and naturally I have gravitated to ones that speak to me personally, so I am aware that others may have valid definitions that could be quite different from the ones described here.

BEING IN TOUCH

A good place to start for a better understanding of contemporary spirituality is with Jon Kabat-Zinn. He is someone who has succeeded in maintaining a prominent position across several different communities, including the academic and scientific domains as well as the world of contemporary spirituality. His success at this may be due, in part, to the fact that, as much as he can, he avoids using the word "spiritual." As he explains in *Wherever You Go, There You Are*: "It's just that I have a problem with the inaccurate, incomplete, and frequently misguided connotations of that word." It is his concern about the possible misinterpretations of the word "spiritual" that make him a particularly good source for attempting to understand it.

Kabat-Zinn directs much of his attention to bringing the ancient Buddhist practice of mindfulness meditation to American audiences. Mindfulness is about paying attention in a nonjudgmental way, examining who we are, questioning how we see the world, and appreciating the richness and vitality of each moment. "Most of all," according to Kabat-Zinn, "it has to do with being in touch." For him, mindfulness is "the direct opposite of taking life for granted."

He believes that mindfulness is not really related to religion except in the most fundamental way, "as an attempt to appreciate the deep mystery of being alive and to acknowledge being vitally connected to all that exists." In spite of his objections, he does reluctantly offer a definition of spirituality: "Perhaps ultimately, spirituality simply means experiencing wholeness and interconnectedness directly, a seeing that individuality and the totality are interwoven, that nothing is separate or extraneous."

He provides some important caveats, however, so as to avoid some of the misguided connotations that he refers to. He reminds us of the damage that can come at any time in history when people become attached to their own view of spiritual truth, as well as the ease with which spirituality can end up fueling self-deception and grandiosity. He also warns against the trap of becoming wedded to "the idea of transcendence" and how easy it is, especially for young people, to get caught up in a quest for "spiritual unity" as a way to bypass some of the necessary hardships and responsibilities of life.

SPIRITUALITY AS ALIVENESS

I would like to return again to the wisdom of Brother David Steindl-Rast. He is both a poet and a philosopher, and, more specifically, a philosopher who focuses on understanding subjective personal experience. For Brother David, all spirituality begins with our own experience as the source of our deepest knowing. Possibly Brother David's greatest contribution is that he articulates age-old spiritual and religious themes in a fresh, new, experiential language that can bring them alive for today's audiences. And because he is not focusing on belief systems or religious doctrines, his message can appeal equally to those across a wide spectrum—from those who identify with a particular religious tradition to those who consider themselves spiritual but not religious, as well as to many who might object to the word "spiritual" but nonetheless resonate with Brother David's teachings.

Brother David describes spirituality at its most basic level as "aliveness." What I like about the word "aliveness" is that it implies that the goal of spirituality is to become more of who we are, not less. This is in contrast to the idea (which is sometimes associated with Eastern religion) that we need to tame or eliminate our egos or other aspects of ourselves that are not "spiritually correct." Spirituality is not about trying to change ourselves. It is more about strengthening that part in each of us that is able to see ourselves and everything around us with the greatest possible clarity—and, in doing so, we have the opportunity to become more alive.

To be alive you must first feel, and being in touch with ourselves and with our feelings is an essential aspect of spirituality. Even though we use the term "mindfulness," this should not imply that "fullness" is just of the mind. Brother

David believes that spirituality is about our complete experience, which very much includes our bodies as well as our minds.

ALIVENESS AND BELONGING

Yet not every kind of aliveness would be considered spiritual. Brother David has in mind a particular kind of aliveness, an aliveness that represents a fullness of the mind, body and spirit. For him, this fullness has everything do to with a sense of belonging. In "Spirituality as Common Sense" he describes true aliveness as "the expression of a profound belonging," something we know "in our bones," even if only for an instant.

For me, the word "belonging" perfectly captures what it feels like to be in relationship with the infinite. We are not alone or alienated when we know that we belong, even though this feeling can be subtle and not something that we always have access to. It may not be clear exactly what we belong to, possibly that overall big thing that is life. All the elements of the world and the universe are alive. It can be exciting to be aware of the aliveness that we share. Brother David reminds us that there is a place for us in this universe and invites us to find our place of belonging.

In "The Price of Peace," Brother David points out that when you look at the heart of every religious tradition, "the starting point in each is the profound limitless sense of belonging." This is the essential element that unites them all. One does not need to believe in a personal God in order to feel a sense of belonging. While the concept of God may be used in religion as the "reference point for that sense of belonging," he emphasizes that the belonging that you experience inside comes first, not "something you find out there."

SPIRITUALITY AS HARMONIZING

One of my favorite definitions of spirituality that incorporates these same themes of unity and belonging is attributed to American psychologist and philosopher William James. He conceptualizes generic religion or spirituality in a way that is simple and easy to remember, but at the same time is profound. We can think of spirituality as "the attempt to be in harmony with an unseen order of things." As with the Tillich definition of faith, there is no specific reference to the content of faith; Tillich refers to the infinite, while James refers to "an unseen order of things."

It is not clear at any given moment whether this unseen order is benevolent or threatening or neutral, but when we are "in harmony," there is always an element of beauty as well as belonging. The melody may not always be beautiful, but singing in harmony always evokes a kind of beauty. Having faith is not about being passive, but rather is very much about being in an active and ongoing relationship with this unseen order. Rather than just listening, we are joining in with the song. We cannot always be in harmony, but, as James says, we can attempt to be.

CONCLUSIONS

Using words to describe the feeling of spirituality can only have meaning to the extent that these words resonate with our own experience and imaginations. Brother David introduces the word "belonging," which helps to capture what is so rewarding about a spiritual orientation—that we can feel a sense of belonging, possibly a "profound belonging" with our world, even if just in certain moments.

Human things must be known to be loved: but Divine things must be loved to be known.
—BLAISE PASCAL

For me, the concept of unity does not come alive without words like "belonging" and ultimately the word "love." As Blaise Pascal so beautifully puts it, how do we feel that we know the divine if not through love? As we come to love more of life, the animals, insects, plants, trees, sky, dirt, rocks, water, even other people, this enhances our sense of gratitude and feelings of belonging. When we feel that we belong, there is no question that we are in a relationship with the infinite and that we are not alone. At any given moment we can always ask ourselves, "Am I feeling in harmony with an unseen order of things?"

THREE SOURCES OF FAITH FOR PSYCHOTHERAPISTS

In befriending life, we do not make things happen according to our own design. We uncover something that is already happening in us and around us and create conditions that enable it.
—RACHEL NAOMI REMEN
My Grandfather's Blessings

When a client initially comes to therapy they may not have much faith. They may have attempted for quite some time to solve their problems on their own, and the admission that they need to reach out to another person, a stranger, for help is not something that they are necessarily proud of. But they feel up against a brick wall, and their own efforts to improve the situation are clearly not working, so they come in, sometimes reluctantly and sometimes with relief that they have finally become willing to reach out for help. It is up to the therapist to have faith in psychotherapy and to have the confidence that, most of the time at least, the client will come to see the benefits.

But it is common knowledge these days that psychotherapists do not have magical solutions to people's problems; even though some clients think that we will give them answers that will set it all straight, most people know that psychotherapy is more of a "process" that cannot be so easily described. True, we help clients recognize counter-productive patterns and we often suggest alternative ways of thinking or behaving that might be more constructive, but the reality is that effecting meaningful change in people's lives is rarely that simple.

The question is, what is there about this "process" of psychotherapy that therapists have faith in, aside from our ability to make suggestions and to educate clients about psychological concepts and theories? What gives us the strength and conviction to presume to take on the daunting task of helping another person overcome obstacles, heal and grow? And how is all of this tied in with spirituality?

PSYCHOTHERAPISTS AS "FACILITATORS"

If we were to ask a beginning psychotherapist where they place their faith, certainly their knowledge base, theories and specific therapeutic skills would be cited as very important. But as we gain experience, it would not take long before most therapists would emphasize their faith in infinitely complex and mysterious processes that appear to have a life of their own. Rather than direct these processes, it would be more accurate to say that we participate in these processes along with the client. We don't so much direct as act as guides or facilitators.

The essence of the connection between psychotherapy and spirituality is that we as therapists rely so heavily on human processes that are, in fact, just as unfathomable, just as infinitely intricate, and just as mysterious as the universe itself. If we think of infinity as reflected only in the endless expanse of the cosmos, then spirituality may not appear to have that much to do with the practice of psychotherapy. But if we think of infinity as a quality that characterizes life itself, including the infinite complexity of our human interactions, then psychotherapists are very much on the front line. One might even say that psychotherapy is an act of faith by Tillich's definition; every day when we go in to work it is our business to be "grasped by and turned towards the infinite."

I have chosen to highlight three of these human processes that are essential ingredients for most psychotherapy and certainly for all types of experiential psychotherapy. They are 1) the "developmental thrust," or the human tendency to move forward in the direction of healing and growth; 2) the healing power of relationship, and 3) the potential of loving compassion to bring about moments of transformation. Each of these three processes could be considered to have a spiritual dimension in that they all transcend our rational understanding; they represent forces of nature that we very much need to work with, but the source of their healing power is a mystery, and they cannot be readily harnessed to work on our schedules or according to our wills.

At one level these processes are so basic and so much a part of our humanity that we often can take them for granted, even as therapists. And yet they are the powerful engines behind so much of what we do in psychotherapy, even if much of their magic happens outside of our conscious awareness. If we as therapist fail to be in alignment with these dynamic sources of healing, it is difficult to imagine a successful outcome with our clients.

THE DEVELOPMENTAL THRUST

If we believe in a "developmental thrust," that humans have an innate tendency to seek growth and actualization, then psychotherapy becomes a much different enterprise than if the therapist is expected to do all the work themselves. This does not mean, of course, that there are no challenges to this growth tendency; people also tend to want to avoid confronting difficult aspects of their lives, and counter-productive belief systems developed at an early age can be quite entrenched. Yet under the right circumstances, when the therapist is able to show sufficient understanding and acceptance, clients are often able to experience this actualizing tendency. The human organism appears to have its own intricate direction. It may not be possible for psychotherapists to anticipate in advance exactly the way it will unfold, but we can do our best to help this growth process along.

What is the mechanism that provides people with this sense of direction or inner certitude? How do we recognize when we are on the right path? Key to understanding the developmental thrust is the sense that there is something inside of us that is not exactly conscious but that "knows" what is meaningful. We can check in with this "inner referent" (or what philosopher and psychotherapist Eugene Gendlin calls a "felt sense") to see if we are on track and to recognize on a moment by moment basis which words or which interactions are moving us in a forward direction. It should be emphasized that moving in a forward direction is not the same thing as just moving in a direction that feels good or pleasant, since much of psychotherapy is actually about finding forward movement by facing areas that are difficult or painful but that ultimately feel very right to explore.

Both the client and the therapist depend upon this felt sense (both our own and the client's) as possibly the most important basis for guiding the psychotherapy process. Even though we as therapists are always heartened when we see that a client's life is improving in a general way, what gives us the most faith in psychotherapy is all those specific moments when the sense of meaning and forward movement is palpable, for both the therapist and the client. Because so much of what is meaningful comes to us in a visceral way that is not directed by our rational agendas, I call this process of finding meaning and forward movement "the miracle of felt meaning."

THE PSYCHOTHERAPY RELATIONSHIP

The client's view of the relationship is the trump card in therapy outcomes...Clients who rate the relationship highly are very likely to be successful in achieving their goals. Despite how chronic, intractable or "impossible" a case may appear, if the client's view of the relationship is favorable, change is more likely to occur.
—MARK HUBBLE, BARRY DUNCAN, SCOTT MILLER
The Heart and Soul of Change: What Works in Therapy

The healing power of relationship is equally miraculous. True, we have rational explanations for why the relationship between the therapist and the client is so integral to successful psychotherapy. We understand that the appreciation and empathic understanding of the therapist is necessary for the client to feel safe to explore unexpressed parts of themselves, and that the therapist can perform a re-parenting function and offer some of what the original parent was unable to give.

But we can look at the same process and use words that are more dramatic and more poignant to describe what is going on. For example, what happens when a client walks into the therapist's office for the first time and looks into the eyes of this human being who is there to help them—that in itself can be such a profound experience that it brings many clients to tears. It is the human interaction that creates the conditions for meaning and for healing to take place in psychotherapy, but why this is the case and exactly how that works is certainly a mystery. Over time, the power of the psychotherapy relationship lies in the accumulation of all of these shared moments of meaning, both large and small.

And there is always the subject of love, and how it is quite common in psychotherapy for therapist and client to experience moments of belonging together that feel like a kind of pure love. The ability of love to heal is one of life's greatest wonders. It is said that what many of us missed as children was "the gleam in the mother's eye." And while we as therapists would like to be able to provide that special gleam for our clients, this is not something that we can accomplish simply through an act of will. It requires that we are able to do a kind of dance with the client where we are somehow coordinated together in a special way.

THE POTENTIAL FOR TRANSFORMATION

And finally, there is the potential for transformation, something that can give a special sense of expectant excitement to our work. People often wonder why psychotherapists are not brought down or discouraged by having to deal throughout the day with people's problems. And yet, to the contrary, our work is often uplifting. So much about psychotherapy is counterintuitive, one example of this being that those times when our clients report the greatest suffering or upheaval in their lives often present the greatest opportunity for healing and growth. When clients are truly brought to their knees, when they have reached the point where they are willing to surrender some of their control and reveal parts of themselves that feel painful, foreign or shameful, real transformation often takes place.

What happens in transformational moments can feel surprising, and yet it is a phenomenon that most therapists are quite familiar with and is really an extension of the concept of felt meaning to a particular type of situation. When a client reveals a difficult truth or speaks from a deep place within themselves, it is often accompanied by an experience of loving compassion and acceptance that offers a special kind of healing and protection. Clients often describe a sense of release and/or relief. Both therapist and client experience the emotional shift, and the feelings of compassion and acceptance are often very present in the room.

Even though the therapist's compassion is essential in these moments, the therapist does not create the moment. It would be more accurate to say that the compassionate therapist is able to actively participate in the moment and help facilitate it. These experiences can be quite dramatic, but the same elements of surrender and relief can be found in many more subtle moments that embody this same transformational quality. It is the sum of these transformational moments, combined with other moments of meaning (in the context of the psychotherapy relationship), that work together to help the client create a vision for change as well as the motivation for change. And, of course, change is also occurring in the psychotherapy process itself, since the client is also a different person as a result of these interactions.

CONCLUSIONS

Whether to call these processes "spiritual" is a matter of semantics, but what is clear is that these healing processes that we rely on in psychotherapy are best described in the philosophical language of complexity theory or chaos therapy as opposed to the traditional, linear scientific concepts that we are more accustomed to. Complexity theory emphasizes the importance of infinitely complex systems of interaction as the foundation of our existence, and the same could be said of psychotherapy. At its foundation, healing in psychotherapy takes place in many moments that are infinitely complex and ultimately cannot be separated from the interaction of the two people involved.

INTEGRATING PSYCHOTHERAPY AND SPIRITUALITY

Values need to have a life-enhancing, energy giving, forward-moving effect. If they push a person's energy back, they are not being used in an experientially sound way.

—EUGENE GENDLIN
Focusing-Oriented Psychotherapy

Fortunately we as therapists do not have to place all of our faith in ourselves, our unique personalities and our accumulated psychological wisdom. Instead, we can place much of our faith in our ability to harmonize with the healing forces of nature. Of course we do not always succeed, but we are seeking to participate in dynamics that go well beyond our more concrete psychotherapy tools and skills. We must be able to access and trust a kind of "knowing" that involves more than just our thinking brains.

To illustrate, if the therapist intends to work with a client's inherent process of forward movement, we must be precisely attuned on a moment by moment basis to the client's experience of felt meaning. We need to be sensitive enough to help the client move forward in the particular way that works for them. And if we wish to create a healing relationship that can include moments of a pure type of love, we must be in harmony with the all that is happening at both the conscious and unconscious levels between the two of us at a given point in time. The same is true if we want to participate in transformational moments. We must really feel our loving compassion in those instances when a client is expressing themselves from their most vulnerable, painful, or shameful places; our reactions must be automatic and completely authentic.

Training programs encourage us to be empathic and attentive, but the real ability to feel aligned with these mysterious healing processes must originate in who we are as people and will be a function of our own personal evolution. This is not about whether we believe in a personal God or whether we call ourselves religious or spiritual. It may be more about the type of relationship that we have established with the infinite aspects of life itself.

INCORPORATING THE SPIRITUAL EMOTIONS

So much of a therapist's skill comes through in the way that we navigate moment by moment—what we pick up on, our body language, when we smile, how we ask questions or encourage the client to go deeper. We have our own felt sense that helps guide us in our navigation process. Our inner navigation systems are very much influenced by our values and our passions, and, for many of us, the spiritual emotions play a major role in guiding our behavior when we are sitting across from our clients.

It follows that if our relationship with the infinite leads us to feel more present to the fullness and possibilities that each moment holds, or to feel more alive in body, mind and spirit, then these qualities can assist us in our therapeutic endeavors. And if we know, in moments, the deep sense of belonging that Brother David describes that resides at the heart of our aliveness, this can help to ground us. If we have reached the point where we understand the virtuous cycle of faith, where we have identified aspects of life that can restore our souls and have made some attempt to prioritize these experiences, this can strengthen our access to the emotional states that we associate with spirituality.

Rather than thinking of therapists as trying to make clients more spiritual, we might define spiritually-oriented therapists as those who are able to cultivate the spiritual emotions in the psychotherapy process. What matters is whether the spiritual emotions come alive in a way that promotes growth and healing for the client. For example, does the therapist's love and compassion help the client feel safer and more fully understood? Is the therapist's sense of awe developed in such a way that they can better respond to the possibilities in the moment? Can the therapist's joy and gratitude enliven the therapy and make for a closer relationship between therapist and client?

INTEGRATING OTHER FUNCTIONS

This does not mean, of course, that we always behave in a loving or overtly compassionate or joyful manner, which could be extremely annoying. It is not enough for a therapist to be passionate about the spiritual emotions. If we are to help our clients, we must have the flexibility to create the kind of interactions with them that are healing, and this is far more complex than just having access to positive feelings. The spiritual emotions and the values that go with them are only appropriate under the right circumstances. Certainly the last thing that we want to do is to impose our values on our clients in a way that is counterproductive.

We must integrate a complex mix of skills if we are to create a successful psychotherapy relationship. The therapist needs to be flexible enough to be fully present with the client as they experience joy, pain, humor, sadness and excitement. Yet to do this effectively the therapist must also be able to set appropriate boundaries and stay grounded and constructive in the face of fear, anger, anxiety, despair, and other difficult emotions that a client may experience. Ideally, we make room for feelings like anger and hopelessness while maintaining the ability to tap into the uplifting spiritual emotions when the time is right.

Much of the therapist's skill requires the integration of the use of the spiritual emotions with all of the other functions that we take on. When it comes to felt meaning, for example, we are not just in a state of limitless awe, listening for and responding to whatever touches our hearts. Most of us come in to every session with our own theories, agendas and ways of conceptualizing a client's problems. Our challenge as spiritually-oriented therapists is to balance our rational agendas with a commitment to remain open and to prioritize what might emerge unexpectedly in a session. But if we are successful in integrating these seemingly competing approaches, we will behave very differently than if we become caught up in our own preconceived ideas and close off the aliveness of the process.

REINFORCING OUR FAITH

Faith is something that evolves over the course of our careers as we repeatedly witness what works and what doesn't work, and as we become more adept in all aspects of our roles. With experience we are rewarded with a multitude of examples of the healing processes in action, and our faith can deepen as a result. We witness the many times when, working together, we are able to help our clients find meaning and experience a sense of forward movement in what seem like stuck places. And we see repeatedly how clients who take the risk of sharing unexplored parts of themselves can open up feelings of love and compassion that make it absolutely clear that the risk was worthwhile.

Over time, therapists also gain solid evidence that we as imperfect individuals are nonetheless capable and worthy of taking on the role of healer and guide. We find that when we have good intentions, hold our boundaries, stay constructive during the darker times, and remain accepting (at least somewhat) of our own imperfections, we can develop powerfully healing relationships. We find that it is possible to experience many moments of a pure type of love with our clients, and that these loving feelings can co-exist along with all of the other feelings that humans would expect to encounter.

CONCLUSIONS

I propose two ways of conceptualizing how psychotherapy and spirituality are related. First, the fact that therapists are attempting to coordinate with the healing forces of nature is, in itself, a type of spiritual act. If we think of spirituality as "the attempt to harmonize with an unseen order of things," then psychotherapy could qualify as a spiritual practice. The unseen order that we deal with involves the mysteries of human growth and development rather than the mysteries of the origins of the universe, but that does not make it less wondrous.

The second way that spirituality relates to our work is that the qualities that we associate with spirituality are also essential to us as therapists. The ability to be present in the moment, to capture the fullness and vitality of the "now," is central to both spirituality and psychotherapy. If we as therapists have been successful in developing our own spiritual emotions, then it is likely that we can bring these emotions alive at appropriate times with our clients. The therapy process itself serves as a ritual that connects us with our own and with our client's spiritual emotions, which can deepen our spirituality. This often feels like a virtuous cycle of faith.

The 23rd Psalm tells us that we can lie down in green pastures and find still waters. We can discover our "path of righteousness," not in the negative sense of righteousness, but in a positive sense of trusting that we are held and protected by the power of something that embodies goodness. I believe that most therapists count on this affinity or partnership with goodness to help give us the strength that we need, even if we are not directly conscious of it. Knowing that we have positive intentions is an excellent start, but we count on something else as well. We count on the experience of actually feeling aligned with these positive forces, which is more than just an intellectual recognition of our intentions. When we feel aligned with the natural healing forces and can sense and be guided by a kind of visceral knowing, then this becomes the ultimate experience of faith.

THE IMPORTANCE OF DOUBT

In the middle of the road of my life I awoke in the dark wood where the true way was wholly lost.
—DANTE ALIGHIERI
The Divine Comedy

So far I have been focusing on the inspiring aspects of faith, but what about its counterpart, the doubting component? If we fail to also acknowledge the presence of doubt in our lives, the times when we feel "wholly lost," then words of faith can quickly become meaningless and ultimately alienating—as if they were meant for other people who have their lives more "together." The reality is that so much of the time we are not inhabiting this faithful place. Instead we are lost, seeking but not finding, struggling, worried, overwhelmed, out of touch, or otherwise preoccupied with our daily concerns and challenges.

As memorable as it is, the 23rd Psalm does not begin to capture the full complexity of the actual human experience. For most of us, the journey is not just about being guided to still waters and green pastures and resting there happily for the remainder of our lifetimes, knowing that we will dwell in the house of the Lord forever. Often we are not feeling fully alive in body, mind and spirit, and we do not always have access to that feeling of belonging that reminds us of the unity of all things and of our place in that universal belonging. We may have experienced faith and even believe that our path is guided, to some degree, by the wisdom that we have accumulated over the course of our lives, but for some of the time, at least, the feelings of love and the other spiritual emotions are nowhere to be found.

This is very true of psychotherapy as well. As much as therapists may have faith in the healing forces of nature, this does not guarantee that we will always be able to access these healing forces in our work or that they will be able to help us along in every situation. Just as there are meaningful and transformational times in psychotherapy, there are also plenty of times when therapy feels stuck, where there seem to be few if any moments of meaning (not to mention transformational moments), and where the psychotherapy relationship, even if it is solid, does not feel sufficient to inspire or to help a client move forward. It is hard to imagine any therapist who would not feel "wholly lost" at times in their work.

DISORIENTATION IS LEGITIMATE

It is helpful for therapists to actively experience faith, but we also need to learn to be skillful in our times of doubt, to know how to be with our clients when the path is not clear and when our inner knowing does not feel sufficient to guide us. Key to doing this is to begin by remembering that doubt is not some horrible enemy threatening to derail our process, but rather is something to be expected. After all, doubt is not the opposite of faith; it is an aspect of faith. Because therapists are working in the realm of faith rather than the realm of certainty, we are to some degree separated from the content of our faith, as Tillich described. If we think of the content of our faith as involving our connection to the healing forces of nature, then it is clear that therapists should not expect to have the sense of control that certainty could offer.

A good way to illustrate how we as therapists are separated from our objects of faith is to think about what happens when we are trying to harmonize with a client's experience of felt meaning. Unlike the old way of thinking, where therapists would assume that their insights and interpretations were correct, we are now more humble and attempt to make interpretations that the client finds meaningful and that create a sense of forward movement. As a result, our interpretations become mere hypotheses until proven otherwise. We must be flexible enough to alter our hypotheses based upon client responses, which will always reflect each client's unique intricacy, beyond anything that we could ever precisely anticipate.

As we become experienced as therapists, it becomes easier to see this process of trial and error as more of a friend than an enemy. With experience we are less likely to interpret our times of confusion or disorientation as meaning that we are not doing therapy correctly or that we are failing to have a sufficient understanding of a particular client. Rather than have it be a signal of a problem, that familiar disoriented feeling can be a friendly reminder that reality is more complex than we can imagine and that we have to take in new information and regroup. We can expect to follow a kind of rhythm of creating structure, dismantling (to various degrees) what we have created, and restructuring.

Once we know that doubt is not the enemy, we are in a position to accept ourselves and our process in times of doubt, just as we attempt to accept and appreciate our clients in difficult moments. We can still make efforts to help a stuck interaction come alive again, but ideally we can do this without conveying a sense of urgency. Having patience is essential for therapists; we do not want to feel anxious about making progress, and we certainly do not want to impose our anxiety or frustrations on the client. This is particularly challenging for beginning therapists who do not fully understand the rhythms of faith and doubt in our work and who may be too quick to blame themselves (or worse, the client) for not being able to move the process forward.

INCLUDING BOTH FAITH AND DOUBT

If the poetry of spirituality only highlighted the uplifting aspects of faith, it may end up being more off-putting than reassuring. By contrast, if we are able to feel met and appreciated right where we are, in our place of doubt, discomfort, despair or alienation, then we are more likely to experience an emotional shift. Like everyone else, psychotherapists need a source of inspiration that speaks to our doubting side. This may be especially true for our profession, since the various advocates of different psychotherapy approaches tend to emphasize their successes and to ignore failures or instances when their approaches are not working.

I find that some of the most beautiful poetry of spirituality addresses this place of no faith and offers ways to re-frame our experience; it helps us to open the door to the unexpected. The segment below is an excerpt from the Mary Oliver poem "Wild Geese" and speaks to that complex mix of faith and doubt that is so much a part of the human experience. Just as the 23rd Psalm celebrates the uplifting qualities of faith, Mary Oliver's poem introduces the possibility of finding some way to belong, even in more troubled times.

Tell me about your despair, yours, and I will tell you mine.
Meanwhile the world goes on.
Meanwhile the sun and the clear pebbles of the rain
are moving across the landscapes,
over the prairies and the deep trees,
the mountains and the rivers.
Meanwhile the wild geese, high in the clean blue air,
are heading home again.
Whoever you are, no matter how lonely,
the world offers itself to your imagination,
calls to you like the wild geese, harsh and exciting
over and over announcing your place
in the family of things.

—MARY OLIVER
Excerpt from "Wild Geese"

"Wild Geese" is not about the profound experience of belonging that Brother David describes as being at the heart of our feelings of aliveness. Instead, it touches on a different kind of belonging that may happen when we are not feeling as connected or inspired. The poem suggests the possibility of finding our place in the family of things, but doing so from a state of loneliness. The world can feel "harsh," like the harsh call of the wild geese, but it can be exciting at the same time. It suggests that we might hear the world calling to us to belong, even in the darker times.

THE TRANSITION FROM DOUBT TO FAITH

When we look at faith and doubt together, we have the advantage of being able to focus on something very critical to humanity, and that is the transition from doubt to faith.

Given the demands of our day to day existence, our ordinary lives don't necessarily inspire faith, and, as a result, we tend to seek some ritualized way to rekindle the experience of faith. I believe that it is this transition to faith that most of us are looking for when we attend church or synagogue or maintain connection with our spiritual communities or spiritual literature.

In the same way, we as psychotherapists are often challenged to make this same transition, to move more into a place of faith and out of our everyday mindset. So much of what we do depends up our ability to make the transition from doubt, fear, preoccupation or indifference to faith. The poem below by David Whyte helps us experience how, in just an instant, we can begin to open the door to faith.

I want to write about faith,
about the way the moon rises
over cold snow, night after night,

faithful even as it fades from
fullness, slowly becoming that last
curving and impossible sliver of
light before the final darkness.

But I have not faith myself,
I refuse it the smallest entry.

Let this then, my small poem
like a new moon, slender and
barely open, be the first prayer
that opens me to faith.

—DAVID WHYTE
"Faith"

In the poem "Faith" the narrator admires how the moon can remain faithful, even in its cycle of fading. The moon is such a good soldier; it loyally "rises over cold snow night after night" until it gradually disappears into "the final darkness." Yet for people, our times of fading are rarely met with faith; we are more likely to feel critical of ourselves, discouraged or frightened in those fading times. We always want to shine at our brightest, although we know intellectually that all of nature, including human nature, must be subject to the cycles of fullness and fading and ultimately of birth and death.

What I like best about the poem is that the narrator takes a stand (just like Dante's hero who is lost in the dark wood) and is willing to admit that he has no faith himself, that he refuses it "the smallest entry." In making that statement to the world, he is acknowledging and, in a way, actually embracing his place of no faith. He reminds us that we can be blessed in this place of no faith, and from there we can still offer a prayer. He writes a poem about the faith of the moon, and this helps to inspire him. With his "small poem, like a new moon, slender and barely open," he offers a first prayer to open himself to faith.

KEEPING HOPE ALIVE

Having experienced faith is an advantage for us when we encounter the inevitable times of doubt in our work. A crucial part of a therapist's faith is not just about accessing the miraculous healing processes, but also being able to trust ourselves and our process, even when we are not feeling connected to our faith and the healing powers do not seem to be present. An important part of what makes psychotherapy feel like a spiritual practice is our role in keeping the hope and possibilities alive when the therapy is less dramatic or expansive.

We need to know how to work with both our faith and our doubt because ultimately we serve as "keepers of the flame" for our clients. We provide a special kind of holding environment to protect our clients and the two of us together during the more fading times when our faith cannot shine enough to guide the way. With the help of our clients, we can continue to hold hope that something might emerge that will surprise us and open up unexpected possibilities, no matter how subtle, for carrying life forward.

Fortunately we have an excellent ritual for returning ourselves to a place of faith, and that is through our experience with our clients. Just as the moon is inspiring, we often find that, in the course of our working day, and often in the course of the minute to minute interactions with our clients, we receive the inspiration that we need. Just a subtle "ah-ha" moment, as when the client speaks a particular phrase that captures just what they are feeling, can make a big difference. Similarly, a moment in an otherwise uneventful session when we might see the innocence in a client's eyes, or when we are able to laugh together, can feel like that prayer that opens us to faith.

LOVE

THE CONFUSION ABOUT LOVE

The best and most beautiful things in the world cannot be seen or even touched. They must be felt with the heart.
—HELEN KELLER

Love is such a powerful word. Maybe it is because of its scope and power that the definition of love seems to elude us. With one word we are attempting to describe the pure, sublime kind of love that is "felt with the heart," as well as the more tempestuous romantic love that can start out as beautiful but can end up causing pain and disappointment. As many of us have learned the hard way, these two types of love often take entirely different forms.

In contrast to the often fickle romantic love of infatuation, the pure love of the heart that Helen Keller refers to only enriches. Pure love has no downside; it does not produce equivalent lows or crashes. Instead of feeling like we are taking from a limited supply, pure love feels infinite—its supply seems to expand the more we experience it. This pure version of love is described in the Corinthians verse from the Bible that is a favorite at weddings but is always worthy of repeating:

Love is patient, love is kind. It does not envy.
It does not boast, it is not proud. It is not rude,
it is not self-seeking, it is not easily angered,

it keeps no record of wrongs. Love does not delight in evil but rejoices with the truth. It always protects, always trusts, always hopes, always perseveres.

This type of love is something that many of us attempt to prioritize in our lives, particularly as we get older and witness over and over again what ultimately sustains us and makes us happy. I imagine that much of what we are doing when we go to church on Sundays or follow a spiritual path or start a spiritual practice such as meditation is that we are looking for a structure, a way to help us get in touch with that pure love that might be difficult to access on our own.

My purpose is to examine the role of the pure type of love in psychotherapy and hope that the reader will be able to make the distinction between pure love and a more self-serving, passionate love. As therapists, we do not want to fall in love in a romantic way with a client. And, if that happens, our professional boundaries should prohibit us from acting this out sexually or allowing our feelings to interfere with our professional roles and the goals of the therapy. But there is always room in therapy for the pure type of love.

THE TABOO TOPIC OF LOVE

American psychologist Carl Rogers has left psychotherapists with a wonderful legacy; when we review how he defined his key concepts of acceptance, empathic understanding and transparency, it is clear that he was describing a real engagement at the deepest human level. He is asking a great deal of the therapist: to create an atmosphere of acceptance and empathic understanding, while at the same time taking the risk of being genuine. Rogers' three concepts have served psychotherapists extremely well over the years.

At the same time, I expect that many therapists have had an experience similar to mine. After my training in the mid 1990's I was very clear about the importance of acceptance and empathic understanding, but less clear about the role of genuineness (how far should we go in being genuine or spontaneous, for example) and less clear even still about the role of love or connection in the psychotherapy process. Of course I knew that the intimacy of passionate attraction was not appropriate, but what about the feelings and expressions of a more pure type of love?

We were taught to offer the client something that felt like unconditional love, yet the loving feelings that might be generated in the process were not directly addressed. Because there was no official professional terminology for describing this fourth dimension, that of connection or intimacy, I was left with some confusion and even guilt about whether real connection or a pure type of love was a legitimate part of psychotherapy. Should therapist and client connect on a deep level, something that might be called a level of the heart or soul, or would acceptance and empathic understanding be best achieved with some professional distance?

LOVE IN PSYCHOTHERAPY

Most experienced therapists have probably come to the same conclusion I have, that real connection in psychotherapy is not only appropriate but also desirable. In fact, I believe that the majority of psychotherapists would agree that psychotherapy is "all about love," particularly longer term therapy. What we mean by that is not so much that the explicit goal of therapy is to help our clients experience more love or to love better, although that is often the case. Rather we are referring to love as something that can be experienced by the client and the therapist as part of the psychotherapy relationship. I am not speaking here about being "in love" in a sexual or romantic way; that is a whole separate topic. My focus is on the feelings of a pure type of love that are often generated in psychotherapy and are frequently an important part of what makes it successful.

Because the word "love" is not accepted as a professional term, there is a facet of our work that goes underground. As a result, some of the beauty of the pure love that we experience in the psychotherapy relationship, along with our sense of the healing power of that love, may not be fully recognized or made explicit. This can leave therapists without the validation and inspiration that might come from feeling free to share our experiences with the larger therapeutic community.

Love is too important a topic in psychotherapy to be ignored or considered politically incorrect. The most challenging part of the learning curve for psychotherapists may be that we are forced to grow as people so as to be more capable of generating a pure type of love in our interactions with our clients. And in order to do this, one of the skills that we must hone over time is the ability to balance moments of intimacy and real connection (that could be called love) with our professional roles and all that that entails. Rather than ignoring the topic of love in psychotherapy, we may be better off as a profession if we take on the challenge directly and teach beginning therapists more about how to achieve this delicate balance: how to maintain professional boundaries while letting our genuine selves and feelings flow through more spontaneously where that is appropriate.

PARAMETERS FOR UNCONDITIONAL LOVE

PSYCHOTHERAPY AND UNCONDITIONAL LOVE

Why do we say that psychotherapy is "all about love"? What about the therapy process generates feelings of love? We begin by looking at the structure of psychotherapy and how the role that the therapist is taking on, if successfully executed, is about as close to a definition of unconditional love as could be imagined. Of course this unconditional love is delivered within very well defined boundaries, taking place within one hour, requiring the therapist to maintain a professional role, and requiring payment by the client. But, in fact, these boundaries are an essential part of what makes it possible for therapists to provide unconditional love. Psychotherapy is an ideal incubator for unconditional love.

The therapist begins with a noble goal, which is to create a relationship with the client that is healing and will foster the client's personal growth. And we as therapists are very much assisted in this endeavor by our appreciation of the client's humanity as well as our recognition of the courage that is required by the client to undertake therapy in the first place. They are choosing you as a guide, as imperfect as you are, and you want to honor their position, protect them, and be worthy of the honor they have bestowed upon you.

There is something sacred about the vulnerability of the client's position. They are asking for help; they have hit a wall in their efforts to address their problems and must be willing to acknowledge the limitations of their power to do it on their own. Ideally the therapist has been in therapy themselves and can convey, over time, that they too have hit walls in their lives and that vulnerability is a shared experience, not something that is just attributed to the client.

ROGERS' THREE DIMENSIONS

In order to make a case that feelings of a pure type of love are desirable in psychotherapy, I believe that we must first step back and look at the characteristics that are associated with a safe and effective psychotherapy relationship. By doing so, it should become more clear why a pure type of love is often generated in this process and, also, how the parameters of the therapist's role can help protect both therapist and client from the wrong type of involvement.

What are the qualities that characterize a good psychotherapy relationship? To answer this I turn to psychologist Carl Rogers, whose writings and lectures in the 1940's, 50's and 60's capture the essence of the ideal helping relationship more succinctly than anything written since. In identifying the three key components of a helping relationship, Rogers has given us a type of formula or mantra that is deeply ingrained in the way most therapists today approach their work:

> *Thus, the relationship which I have found helpful is characterized by a sort of transparency on my part, in which my real feelings are evident; by an acceptance of this other person as a separate person with value in his own right; and by a deep empathic understanding which enables me to see his private world through his eyes.*
> —CARL ROGERS
> *On Becoming a Person*

Unlike some other psychotherapy traditions that focus on the power of the therapist's interpretations, Rogers believed that, in the safety of the right relationship, the client will find a way to use the relationship for growth and change, and that this is how personal development in psychotherapy occurs. Research results support Rogers' conclusions; the vast research in our field increasingly confirms the view that, aside from inherent client strengths, the quality of the psychotherapy relationship is the most powerful factor in predicting successful therapy outcomes, much more so than any technique or the orientation or education of the therapist.

Rogers did not use the word "love" to describe his approach, but his three components, when combined, could be said to describe the essence of unconditional love in psychotherapy. Over time, more therapists have come around to his way of thinking. In an extensive poll by *Psychotherapy Networker* magazine, over 2,500 psychotherapists were asked, "Over the last 25 years, which figures have most influenced your practice?" The figure with the most votes was Carl Rogers.

While there is a great advantage in being left with Rogers' three key concepts, it is unfortunate that many of us remember only certain words, typically "acceptance," "empathic understanding," "transparency" or "congruence." As helpful as they are as touchstones or markers, over the years they have lost some of their original meaning and power to inspire. So I will include here a summary of Rogers' concepts in the hopes of capturing more of the passion that he intended that they convey.

ACCEPTANCE AND EMPATHIC UNDERSTANDING

In using the word "acceptance," Rogers is not referring

simply to an intellectual attitude of acceptance, but to something that carries genuine feelings of warmth and respect. He describes a therapist's acceptance of the client as "a warm regard for him as a person with unconditional self-worth—of value no matter what his condition, his behavior, or his feelings." Rogers is telling us that the warm regard that he is referring to does not depend upon the client behaving well, nor is it based upon the client's "potential" or who the client "could be." Rather, the acceptance is for the client as he is right now.

Rogers emphasizes "the safety of being liked and prized as a person." Ideally, acceptance is not a resigned stance but an active liking and, in fact, a "prizing." Who would not want to feel prized by their therapist, and for being just the way they are?

But acceptance alone is not enough if it does not also include understanding. Rogers describes a "deep empathic understanding which enables me to see his private world through his eyes." Rogers makes it clear that this is not just about "seeing" in a dispassionate way. Rather, he is suggesting that the therapist resonate in a visceral way with the client's inner experience. And empathic understanding is not something that therapists should keep to themselves; it is necessary for the client to witness the therapist's understanding.

TRANSPARENCY

The biggest challenge, of course, is for the therapist to do all of this while still being genuine, and to also be able to reveal, to some degree, other types of feelings that might seem more problematic. Rogers found that just behaving in an accepting or empathic way could be counterproductive if he was actually feeling something quite different but was afraid to show it. Attempting to be consistently accepting if his feelings were not genuine would ultimately be perceived as "inconsistent or untrustworthy." So he concluded that the attitudes of acceptance and empathic understanding must be balanced with the need to be real. Ideally everything in our expressions and body language should line up with what we are saying. Yet how do we as therapists risk exposing feelings or attitudes to a client that we might not accept in ourselves or that we fear might pose a risk to the psychotherapy relationship?

Rogers believed that if he could be conscious of his own feelings and really accept those feelings, then there was an excellent chance that his relationship with the client would be helpful. Yet he adds that "acceptantly to be what I am, in this sense, and to permit this to show through to the other person, is the most difficult task I know and one I never fully achieve." Nonetheless, this was a challenge that he gladly took on. According to Rogers, "It has meant that if I am to facilitate the personal growth of others in relation to me, then I must grow, and while this is often painful it is also enriching."

A VIRTUOUS CYCLE OF LOVE

In his commitment to create the kind of relationship that his clients can use for their growth, Rogers is advocating a role for the therapist that requires considerable sacrifice, strength, flexibility, generosity, and courage. In order to achieve this we must be willing to put aside our own preferences and agendas and focus on another person's world, something we would not generally do in our non-working lives. In addition to listening attentively, we are constantly forced to reevaluate the maps that we have constructed in our minds to help orient us to what is happening with a particular client, a process that can be humbling and disorienting A therapist also needs the emotional sensitivity, strength and flexibility to be deeply empathic while at the same time maintaining our separate identities and professional roles and boundaries.

Rogers admitted that he needed to grow in order to better accomplish the goals that he outlined. And clearly Roger's experience is not unique. It is difficult to imagine any successful therapist who has not been forced to grow and change as a result of the challenges they face in their work. The way we change can take many forms: we may need to alter our cherished points of view, expand our ability to respect and appreciate others, confront some of our own psychological demons or unfinished business, learn to own and accept aspects of ourselves that have felt wrong or shameful, take certain risks in our work, or, most likely, all of the above. And this willingness on the part of the therapist to grow and to experience the pain that accompanies change is a big part of what generates love in our process. While we may prefer to do much of this growing outside of the view of our clients, they often benefit from witnessing, to some degree, our struggles and involvement.

Whether what Rogers is describing deserves to be called love is a matter of debate, but there is little question that the role he advocates for therapists requires that we behave in a loving manner. And when we behave in a loving manner toward someone, our behavior tends to generate feelings of love, not only in them, but also in us. As the popular songs remind us, love in not just something we take, it is something we make. And when we are able to follow Rogers' advice, we can expect that our clients feel not only accepted and understood, but also, at least on occasion, loved, and that they will respond in kind to our attentiveness and commitment, which feeds back into a virtuous cycle.

A DIFFERENT WAY TO THINK ABOUT LOVE

LOVE AS THE MISSING FOURTH DIMENSION

When therapists say that therapy is "all about love," they are referring to the felt presence of connection between therapist and client in the moment to moment flow of the therapy session. Acceptance and empathic understanding are necessary but not sufficient conditions for describing these types of feelings. It is true that moments of acceptance or empathic understanding can carry a level of intensity that might qualify as moments of real connection, but this is not always the case. We can be appropriately accepting and empathic without necessarily creating a moment of intimacy.

The problem is that without a separate dimension to measure the level of connection, we are unable to fully explicate a crucial dynamic in the therapy process, and one that deserves to be better examined and understood. With Rogers' three dimensions as a foundation for describing a helping relationship, I would like to suggest a fourth dimension: namely, the presence of real connection (or what might be called love) as it occurs in the psychotherapy process.

In order to zero in on this dimension of connection or love, I suggest that we shift from an abstract view to one that examines the micro-moment interactions. While the feelings of love between therapist and client that build over time are crucial to the success of the therapy, looking at the micro-moments offers another valuable perspective that cannot be achieved if we only look at the long-term picture. Rather than ask whether we love the client or the client loves us, we might ask: What qualifies as a moment of love? And what role should these moments play in the psychotherapy process?

WHAT QUALIFIES AS A MOMENT OF LOVE?

I would like to propose a definition of love that is very applicable to the psychotherapy process and that is well suited for describing how feelings of love show up in a given moment. We know that love is there, but we do not have a specific way to recognize it, describe it, or understand its role. My favorite definition of love is from Brother David Steindl-Rast in his book *Gratefulness, the Heart of Prayer:*

> *When we ask for characteristics of love applicable to each and all of its forms, we find at least two: a sense of belonging and wholehearted acceptance of that belonging with all its implications. These two characteristics are typical for every kind of love, from love of one's country to love of one's pets, while passionate attraction is typical only of falling in love. Love is a wholehearted "yes" to belonging.*

Brother David's definition of love is both precise and inclusive. The word "belonging" seems more precise than the word "love" because it describes a particular kind of feeling that is easily recognizable, the feeling of belonging together. When we feel love for a pet, for example, along with that comes a feeling of belonging that is undeniable. The term is not used here to imply any kind of inequity, like a slave belonging to a master, but rather to convey a sense of the rightness of being together.

Brother David's definition is also precise in that it gives us a particular criterion for assessing the presence of love in a given moment in time. Unless we feel "a sense of belonging and a wholehearted acceptance of that belonging with all its implications," then the feeling is not love. It must be a wholehearted "yes" in order to qualify; it must be strong enough to reach that threshold. And, as Brother David says, the feeling of belonging is inclusive enough to apply to all of the forms that love takes, from love of your partner or children to love for a country, friend, idea, piece of music or art, your home, a tree, football team, a poem, etc. This definition can apply to anyone or anything that can be joined through a sense of belonging.

MOMENTS OF BELONGING IN PSYCHOTHERAPY

Therapists can attempt to create an environment of unconditional love, which is an excellent beginning. Yet real moments of belonging require more than just a diligent commitment to the attitudes of acceptance and empathic understanding. We must also take the risk of being spontaneous, at least on occasion, since loving feelings cannot flourish when we are safely or rigidly positioned in a professional role.

Experiencing real connection requires that we be willing to reveal the person (or at least some of that person) behind our roles. And in longer term therapy we often do not have much choice. The therapy process captures so much of who we are as people, with our unique personalities, styles, quirks, strengths and weaknesses. Our facial expressions, how we show our appreciations of our clients or react to their appreciation of us, how we handle ourselves when we are not feeling their appreciation of us—so much of this is outside of our conscious awareness, yet these spontaneous moments can determine whether or how a feeling of belonging takes place.

In psychotherapy this feeling of belonging can happen in any kind of moment. The most obvious example would be a dramatic moment where a client reveals a previously unspoken truth that is laden with emotion and grabs us to the core. As a client speaks from a raw or vulnerable place, it often transports us to our own place of vulnerability, but in a way that feels tender and filled with compassion. A sense of belonging can also arise out of conflict, such as when a client is angry at you and as the two of you struggle with the anger it brings you closer together.

But moments of belonging are not only triggered by dramatic interpersonal interactions. The feeling of belonging can be a moment of humor or spontaneity that takes us beyond our normal boundaries into a realm of togetherness such that we can't help but smile. Or it can be subtle, such as the way it feels when the two of you greet each other or the feelings of connection in an animated intellectual discussion when the ideas just seem to flow. Any way the therapist and client are interacting in the therapy process always has the potential of being one of those special moments where there is the unqualified "yes" to belonging.

THE I-THOU RELATIONSHIP

Another way to define connectedness in a moment in time is the concept of "I" and "Thou" made famous by Austrian philosopher Martin Buber. Buber describes a special connection that joins two people together and is distinguished from the ordinary interactions of everyday life, which he refers to as the I-It way of being. When we are preoccupied with accomplishing our goals, completing tasks and otherwise getting along in our lives, we see others as separate individuals who we either "use" or "experience." But the I that speaks to a Thou suggests an entirely different kind of relatedness.

Man wishes to be confirmed in his being by man, and wishes to have a presence in the being of the other... Secretly and bashfully he watches for a Yes which allows him to be and which can come to him only from one human person to another.

—MARTIN BUBER
"Distance and Relation"

I-Thou moments are moments of genuine meeting and mutuality, where we are no longer two separate individuals but move instead into a relationship that feels more expansive, one where we experience the other person in a more heartfelt and complete way. In the I-Thou relationship we no longer see the other person as an object with particular qualities or characteristics. According to Buber:

When I confront a human being as my Thou and speak the basic word I-Thou to him, then he is no thing among things nor does he consist of things. He is no longer He or She. . . a dot in the world grid of space and time, nor a condition that can be experienced and described, a loose bundle of named qualities. Neighborless and seamless he is then and fills the firmament. Not as if there were nothing but he; but everything else lives in his light.

—MARTIN BUBER
I and Thou

When we as therapists are experiencing our clients as Thou, we are transformed in that moment from our normal way of being in the world. This is not just an interaction where the therapist is using acceptance and deep empathic understanding to help transport the client to a different place. In a true I-Thou moment, the therapist is also transported. As Buber tells us, the person of the Thou "fills the firmament" and "everything else lives in his light." The I of the I and Thou is different from the I of the I and It.

Most therapists would like to think that they are operating more in an I-Thou world than an I-It world with their clients. But I-Thou moments are more rare and transformational than something we could sustain on an ongoing basis. They often come unexpectedly. As much as we make an effort to see our clients in the fullness of who they really are, achieving true I-Thou moments is not something that we have complete control over. In speaking of mutuality, Buber says, "It is a grace for which one must always be ready and which one never gains as an assured possession." So therapists should not think of an I-Thou relationship as a way of being, but more as a moment of grace, an opportunity for which we can be prepared.

WHAT DOES IT MEAN TO LOVE SOMEONE?

Conceptualizing love as something that happens in moments in time avoids the more complicated issue of whether we would claim to love someone as an overall conclusion. I am reminded of couples who tell me, "We love each other, but we are not in love." Now what exactly does that mean? I tend to hear this as equivalent to saying that they care very much about each other but do not have many (or any) moments of that unqualified "yes" to belonging. For most of us, concluding we love someone probably means that there are enough moments where we feel that unqualified "yes" that the conclusion feels justified, even though we do not experience these moments all of the time.

For therapists, it may not be particularly useful to attempt to reach general conclusions about whether we love some or all of our clients. What is more relevant, I believe, is that we have enough moments of belonging with a client, and this provides a reference point for us. Moments of belonging between a therapist and client typically coexist with other moments where the feelings are much less positive, including moments of irritation, boredom, fear, anger, anxiety, etc. But even though there are many other competing feelings and moments that are decidedly not moments of belonging (as is true for even the most loving relationships), that reference point of belonging allows us to find the place within ourselves where there is love for that person.

FINDING A PLACE OF LOVE FOR OUR CLIENTS

As we gain experience over the years, we often witness special moments of belonging with our clients that would have been impossible to predict in advance. There may be clients who we find challenging, and yet we can identify moments with these clients that felt unquestionably like love—moments where we sensed that unqualified "yes." In fact, it is often the most difficult clients who can produce the most intense moments of love. They often force us to be particularly strong, to remain present instead of backing away in fear or a desire to distance ourselves, and these encounters can turn out to be very rewarding. More difficult clients often demand greater intimacy.

Similarly, a moment of love is often not characteristic of an entire session. I have one client where the sessions can feel uninspired, boring, flat, relentlessly negative, and yet there have been moments at the end of such a session where something in her body language or the way she looks at me seems to convey a kind of appreciation and understanding. I sense that she needs to keep me at a distance, at least for now, and when our eyes meet as she is headed out the door, I experience that unqualified "yes." There is no doubt that, in that moment, we belong together. I feel a wholehearted acceptance of our belonging "with all its implications," as Brother David says.

I would make the case that all we need is one real moment of belonging with a client to be able to find a place of love for them. That does not mean that we would necessarily want to actively pursue a friendship with them if we met in the normal course of our lives. (And although we may feel this way about certain clients, it should be noted that our professional boundaries discourage us from turning client relationships into friendships where we venture outside of the regular therapy setting.) But once we have experienced that sense of belonging with a client, we have the ability to draw upon that feeling, at least some of the time, in the course of the psychotherapy relationship.

LOVE AS A SOURCE OF DIRECTION

We are shaped and fashioned by what we love.
—JOHANN WOLFGANG VON GOETHE

PRIORITIZING LOVE

The ability to find wisdom and happiness may depend to a large degree on how successful we are at finding and prioritizing love. Love is not just something to randomly feel and enjoy; it can also offer a source of direction in life if we are able and willing to nurture it and listen to what it wants from us. If we are fortunate, we can say at the end of our lives that we have been "shaped and fashioned by what we love," as Goethe says. But this requires that we have really allowed love to shape and direct us.

When the poet David Whyte recites the Mary Oliver poem "Wild Geese" he keeps repeating one line, with an emphasis on the word "only": "You *only* have to let the soft animal of your body love what it loves." The emphasis is to help us see the word "only" as facetious—as if it were natural to do something so seemingly simple as letting the soft animal of our body love what it loves. It sounds so easy, but allowing this to happen can feel dangerous and ultimately counterintuitive, maybe because it means that we must be in touch with our deepest longings and feelings of vulnerability.

You do not have to be good.
You do not have to walk on your knees
for a hundred miles through the desert, repenting.
You only have to let the soft animal of your body
love what it loves.

—MARY OLIVER
Excerpt from "Wild Geese"

How compelling to think that some soft place in our bodies is craving to love what we love, yet we often do not listen but instead let it atrophy. The obstacle may not be our capacity to feel love, but rather our willingness to access it and nurture it sufficiently to allow it to even begin to reach its seemingly limitless potential as a guiding and comforting force in our lives. We always have the choice to follow our hearts; our hearts are probably our best spiritual guide, more reliable than any prescribed doctrine that would presume to show us the way.

NAVIGATING FROM THE HEART

Knowing that love is something that we can access within ourselves and use to guide our behavior has tremendous implications for psychotherapists, although therapists might not think of it this way. Most of us have learned over the years to evoke, recognize, lift out, encourage, celebrate and otherwise prioritize heartfelt moments in the therapy process. This may sometimes be a conscious choice, but much of this prioritizing happens at a visceral level. I call this source of guidance for therapists "navigating from the heart." Our hearts, the place of love and compassion, listen and respond in a totally different way than if we are listening just with our minds.

Navigating from the heart would certainly include a sensitivity to relational moments, especially feelings of love or belonging between the therapist and client. Most therapists know instinctively to watch the quality and texture of the psychotherapy relationship and to let our hearts respond to the "I-Thou" opportunities or to any other special moments between therapist and client. But navigating from the heart is not limited to relational moments.

We also use our hearts to help us find and recognize moments of meaning. Brother David claims that "the heart is the organ of meaning," something that may at first seem strange, since we often think of the heart as ruling the interpersonal domain and the mind as ruling the domain of ideas and meaning. And yet when something becomes meaningful to us there is an obvious visceral component, a sense of release and rightness. Our heart represents the place of restlessness, the place where we long for meaning and where we recognize and register meaning when it occurs. As Brother David describes it, meaning is the place "where our hearts find rest."

Listening with my heart, I will find meaning. For just as the eye perceives light and the ear sound, the heart is the organ of meaning.
—BROTHER DAVID STEINDL-RAST
A Listening Heart

When the client is exploring their inner world and we are listening wholeheartedly, we use our hearts to help guide the client to find the words, images or feelings that create meaning for them. The search for meaning is something that therapist and client undertake together and feel together. And our ability to experience this comes from the heart, the part of ourselves that we associate with love. So, if we think about it, love plays a role in all aspects of therapy, not just in moments where we are explicitly focused on the psychotherapy relationship. Where there are moments of meaning, the heart is also present and responding. One could say about psychotherapy that there is always love in meaning and always meaning in love.

THE SPIRITUAL DIMENSION OF LOVE

Love is not primarily a relationship to a specific person; it is an attitude, an ordination of character which determines the relatedness of the person to the whole world as a whole, not toward one object of love.
—ERICH FROMM
The Art of Loving

"Love" is a topic of many sermons and is clearly associated with spirituality. Yet we are often more comfortable focusing on the strictly interpersonal dimension of love (in our romantic relationships or with family and friends, for example) as opposed to taking a broader, more spiritual perspective. Even still, I imagine that most of us could relate to Erich Fromm's message, that love is not just about a relationship to a specific person.

LOVE THAT TRANSCENDS THE OBJECT

When we experience moments of love or belonging, are these feelings just directed toward one object of love, or is the experience something more than that? And if we are loving people and practice genuine love in our lives, does that lead to "an ordination of character" that affects our relatedness to the world as a whole? In raising these questions we introduce the spiritual dimension of love—the notion that with a pure type of love we make contact not just with the immediate object of our affections, but also with a whole different dimension of living.

To see love as limited to the object of love diminishes the experience somehow. Maybe that is because love has a transcendent quality; our feelings start with the original object but do not end there. The object serves as a catalyst that transports us to an altogether different state, possibly even deserving to be called a state of grace, where we feel a renewed sense of connection or belonging, not just with the object, but also with ourselves and with the broader world or universe.

I find that the spiritual language captures some of the powerful aspects of the experience of love that might be missed if we limit ourselves to the secular vocabulary. Introducing the spiritual language does not have to suggest any particular religious doctrine or a belief in a personal God. Rather it is an attempt to describe more completely and more fully the actual nature of the feelings that can be associated with love—a phenomenological emphasis as opposed to a religious emphasis. Because the spiritual words are more poignant, they can also feel more precise or accurate.

LOVE AND UNIVERSAL BELONGING

By defining love as an unqualified "yes" to belonging, Brother David does not specifically introduce spiritual language, yet the spiritual implications of his words become clearer when we explore what the word "belonging" means to him. For Brother David, the feeling of belonging with a person or any other aspect of life has the potential to extend further to a feeling of universal belonging. Love is not just about the one object of our love; is also about coming nearer to the experience of ultimate belonging.

What we know at the end of our quest is the meaning of belonging. And the driving force of our spiritual quest is our longing to belong.
—BROTHER DAVID STEINDL-RAST
"The Great Circle-Dance of the Religions"

Many of us come to experience love in this broader way, not just limited to family and friends, but expanding to include more and more. If we are able to feel (in moments at least) a sense of overall belonging to our world or to our universe, that may best represent the ultimate spiritual goal. As Brother David describes in "The God Problem": "It will be a life determined by that deep sense of belonging which softens the rigid boundaries of our small ego and liberates us to experience our oneness with all—with all there is, and with the transcendent 'More' beyond all."

SERVICE AS AN EXPERIENCE OF BELONGING

Adding the spiritual perspective helps to clarify what is actually happening in moments of belonging in psychotherapy. These moments are not just about the feeling of belonging between therapist and client but can also include, at the same time, the sense of belonging with the self and belonging with the world as a whole. The uplifting feelings that result from these moments in psychotherapy are a big part of what makes the process feel hopeful, productive and rewarding—for both the client and the therapist.

If the spiritual quest is about finally coming to know the

meaning of belonging, then creating moments of belonging and expanding who and what we love is an excellent pathway to get there—the way we undertake the journey. Psychotherapy, with its many opportunities for pure love and connection, offers a vehicle for traveling on a spiritual path for clients and therapists alike. So when we think of what is healing for the client, we might include the growth that comes from participating in the many moments of belonging that psychotherapy can provide.

Psychotherapy also offers therapists a vehicle for a spiritual journey. In fact, our entire careers are devoted to putting aside our own needs and agendas and learning to appreciate, understand and connect with a wide range of people, many of whom we never would have befriended in the normal course of our lives. In expanding our ability to love and feel a sense of belonging with a wide circle of people, we ourselves are forced to grow and change at the same time that we are helping our clients to grow.

> *Professionalism has embedded in service a sense of difference, a certain distance. But on the deepest level, service is an experience of belonging, an experience of connection to others and to the world around us. It is this connection that gives us the power to bless the life in others. Without it the life in them would not respond to us.*
> —RACHEL NAOMI REMEN
> *My Grandfather's Blessings*

Ideally, over the course of our careers, we come to understand the meaning of belonging, and this brings us closer to being able to serve at the level that Rachel Naomi Remen describes. When we are engaged in serving at this deep level, it is our sense of belonging (this connection to others and to the larger world) that gives us the power to bless the life in others. We need this connection and the power that it conveys. Otherwise, as she says, the life in our clients "would not respond to us."

COMPASSION

COMPASSION AS BEING TOGETHER WITH SUFFERING

Compassion is that which makes the heart of the good move at the pain of others. It crushes and destroys the pain of others; thus, it is called compassion. It is called compassion because it shelters and embraces the distressed.

—THE BUDDHA

Compassion occurs only between equals.

—THE DALAI LAMA

I found that I could not write about compassion without first having just the right definition of what compassion is. In order to feel grounded in my writing, I needed to find the exact words. I propose that we define compassion as being "together with suffering." If we refer to the Latin roots of "com" meaning "with" we come up with the concept of "co-suffering" or "suffering with." I like the emphasis on the word "with." When we feel compassion we are joined together with the one who is suffering.

This is what ultimately distinguishes compassion from sympathy. With sympathy we are aware of the suffering of the other and feel bad for them, but there is not the same sense of joining with. In fact, sympathy seems to emphasize the gulf between the one who is suffering and the other, as if the sympathetic observer is looking down on the other from a more comfortable or superior position. There is the feeling: "There but for the grace of God go I!" Most of us would not want the sympathy of others, whereas I imagine that compassion would be universally welcomed.

THE HEALING POWER OF COMPASSION

Of the spiritual emotions that I am examining, compassion is the one that reminds us that spirituality is not just about valuing or encouraging positive emotional states. Compassion is the opposite; even though it is possible to alleviate suffering through compassion, we only achieve this by seeking out and joining with the difficult, painful, or vulnerable place, both theirs and our own.

The paradox is that even though compassion is joining with suffering, compassion is not an experience of suffering. It may be more accurate to think of compassion as including both co-suffering and co-passion, with co-passion representing the more complete range of emotions that can be released in the presence of loving compassion. Bringing in compassion makes it possible to transcend suffering and is associated with feelings of safety, intimacy, connection, love and belonging.

Buddha's statement is a tribute to the healing power of compassion; he tells us that compassion can literally crush and destroy the pain of others. The source of its power is that it is a heartfelt experience. As the Buddha says, compassion is "that which makes the heart of the good move at the pain of others." To the extent that compassion comes from the heart, it offers a special kind of shelter to the distressed, and possibly even an embrace. This is the most powerful form of compassion—when we feel met at our place of greatest pain and suffering with a heartfelt embrace.

Why do our hearts respond to the suffering of others? I believe, at some gut level, that we know that the pain of the other is somehow the same as our pain, even though we may it experience it differently. In fact, it is not just the pain of the two of us, but some even bigger, more universal experience of pain or rawness or tenderness that is part of our shared humanity. If we are to connect with another person at the depths of our being, then this connection must include the sensitivity and vulnerability that seem to reside within us at these deepest levels.

A SOLUTION IS NOT AN EMBRACE

Unlike empathy, which can be felt at some distance, the word "compassion" implies a more passionate response that includes an active desire to be involved. If we are sitting home in the comfort of our living rooms, we might feel compassion, but we cannot offer the shelter or the embrace that the Buddha references unless we interact in some way with those who are suffering. Compassion makes us want to reach out.

In the Buddha's definition of compassion, the action that is described is that of joining with or connecting. This is a different emphasis than what might come to mind when we think of compassion for the poor or for people who are sick or starving. In these examples, our desire to reach out may involve taking actions to address the source of the suffering. Our compassion might inspire us to write a check to a charity or to volunteer our time in a third world country to work directly with the poor to help improve their living conditions.

Yet when it comes to psychotherapy, it is very important not to confuse acts to alleviate suffering (such as giving to charity or providing food to the hungry) with the experience of being sheltered in the compassionate embrace. When it comes to psychological or emotional suffering, the irony is that the goal of alleviating suffering by fixing or eliminating it directly is often not the right approach and, in fact, is often exactly the wrong approach. If we remember that compassion is about *being together with* suffering, then that is a completely different goal than attempting to fix or eliminate the suffering, as noble as one's intentions may be.

WHEN FIXING INTERFERES WITH COMPASSION

A classic example of how "fixing" can be counterproductive is that of a typical type of male-female communication. The wife comes home from the office upset about something that happened at work, and the husband goes into brainstorming mode, doing his best to come up with a solution that will help his wife feel better. He offers a suggestion, "What if you told your boss. . . ." Yet much to his dismay, rather than calming down, she becomes increasingly annoyed and agitated. She may even appear angry at him, leading him to exclaim, "But I'm only trying to help!"

She is frustrated because, in this example, she wants compassion as opposed to a solution. She wants to be joined in her suffering—for her husband to validate her feelings and welcome her suffering self. Referencing the Buddha's words, she wants to feel that her husband's heart is moved by her pain. She wants to experience the shelter of his compassion and to have the sense that her husband is embracing her in her time of distress. This is where the power of compassion lies; this is how compassion can crush and destroy the pain of her suffering.

How many husbands (or wives, for that matter) can overcome the natural desire to try to fix the problem and say instead, "I can see why you are upset. This is difficult. I can relate to what you are going through. I'm so glad that you shared this with me rather than just keeping it to yourself." Just as this couple may eventually work together to fix the problem and find a solution, problem solving in this example will not work until they first join together in a compassionate stance.

COMPASSION AND PSYCHOTHERAPY: JOINING VERSUS FIXING

Even when—and it always is—the story is very complex, a willingness to walk together into the deepest circles of the patient's experiential hell characterizes the attitude of compassion or emotional availability that I believe the process of clinical understanding requires.

—DONNA ORANGE
Thinking for Clinicians

The attitude of compassion in psychotherapy is about the willingness of the therapist to welcome and walk together into what Donna Orange refers to as "the deepest circles of the patient's experiential hell." We do not leave our clients alone with their vulnerability, pain, shame, or despair. Rather, we do the opposite and actively befriend that which is shunned, judged, feared, pushed away, and hidden.

When we take the journey together and encourage them to tell their story, we are offering our clients a new kind of "relational home" for all that is associated with their suffering. Sometimes this act in and of itself can produce a distinct emotional shift, as when it "crushes and destroys the pain" like the Buddha proclaims. But the emotional shift does not have to be dramatic for compassion to be healing. Whenever compassion "shelters and embraces the distressed," we can assume that there is always the potential for healing, even in the more difficult or stuck times.

THE ROLE OF THE THERAPIST

I imagine that most psychotherapists are drawn to working with a client's pain and suffering, something that people outside of our field might find surprising or bewildering. But for those of us who feel called to serve in this way, having the opportunity to be with a client's emotional pain can feel like an honor. Ideally we have learned to accept and even cherish that in ourselves which is most capable of suffering. We come to know in a visceral way that our vulnerability is not ours alone but instead is part of a larger human vulnerability.

As therapists, we need to be in touch with our own emotional wounds, including those aspects of ourselves that might embarrass us. Ironically, it is often through our vulnerability that we bond with our clients, not through our sophisticated interventions or the extent of our psychological knowledge or expertise. And in true moments of meeting, it is not just the therapist's compassion that is healing. In these moments, compassion feels more like a force that is present in the room; it is not just something that the therapist brings.

But it would be misleading to imply that all of psychotherapy is a continuously enriching process, filled with genuine moments of bonding based upon the most heartfelt experience of compassion. As therapists, we learn to listen to our hearts when they respond to the pain of others, and to use our natural compassion to help our clients in their process of healing. But when our natural compassion does not feel strong enough to guide us, we can still take on a compassionate attitude; we remember to actively welcome the patient's suffering and pain, since that is the place where they most need us to join with them. Taking on a compassionate attitude helps us to continue to shelter our clients and provide a holding environment, even when their suffering does not present itself in ways that are easy for us to connect with.

BALANCING COMPASSION AND FIXING

Of all the careers that are available to those who feel called upon to exercise compassion, the role of psychotherapist is uniquely suited to compassion as the Buddha defined it—the compassion that is about the direct connection with another person, as opposed to compassion that leads people to perform good works or to focus on correcting wrongs in the world. As psychotherapists, a large part of our role is to "be with" suffering and to facilitate, with the help of our clients, the shelter and embrace of compassion that the Buddha was referring to.

The gesture of joining through compassion is an entirely different gesture than identifying a problem that needs to be solved—a distinction that psychotherapists are intimately familiar with. That is a big part of the difference between looking to a friend for "help" versus seeing a psychotherapist who has been trained to understand how to use compassion in the healing process. While the feeling of compassion may be accessible to many people, the ability to facilitate a compassionate encounter requires considerable sensitivity and the discipline to keep the focus on what the other person needs. Learning to be with our clients in their place of suffering sometimes feels counterintuitive, which is why this can be the most important skill that we develop as psychotherapists.

Yet even after all our training to avoid falling into the "fixing" trap, we still can make the mistake of trying to "fix" suffering at times when it would be more helpful to join it or to gently explore it. This is because the reality is that psychotherapists need to do both—sometimes the joining and sometimes the help with fixing. And the need to balance these two often opposing types of attitudes and interventions can involve a complex dance that takes many years of practice to even begin to master.

WHEN FEELINGS ARE JUDGED TO BE WRONG

We are ultimately in a paradoxical position as psychotherapists. Our clients often come to us looking for help in alleviating their painful feelings. And yet their actual feelings may not be the primary cause of their suffering. What can be a bigger factor is the sense that they shouldn't be feeling what they are feeling. It is often their judgments about their feelings that contribute significantly to their distress. So if we are too eager to help them "get rid of" what they are feeling, it can end up reinforcing these negative judgments. As Pema Chodron points out, once we label our feelings as wrong or as a problem, we set in motion a kind of self-criticism that can be counterproductive.

> *When something hurts in life, we don't usually think of it as our path or as the source of wisdom. In fact, we think that the reason we're on the path is to get rid of this painful feeling... At that level of wanting to get rid of our feeling, we naively cultivate a subtle aggression against ourselves.*
>
> —PEMA CHODRON
> *When Things Fall Apart*

This tendency to judge painful feelings is something that

therapists see often and have many names for. I have heard it referred to as "feelings about feelings" or "the bruise on the broken bone." I call it "the double whammy." Clients often fear that their feelings make them bad, not loveable, defective in some way, and that their pain or suffering will drive others away. This is particularly true where our clients had parents who were not attuned to their painful feeling states, contributing to the conviction that they were not loveable when they were hurt, frightened, insecure, angry, discouraged, lonely, frustrated, anxious, failing or in any other type of distress.

Therapists must always be sensitive to the larger relational dynamics of the moment. It is better to miss an opportunity to help "fix" a problem than to jump in at the wrong time and send the message that the client's feelings or experience is wrong in some way. As therapists, what is most important is to provide   a relational home for the suffering self of our clients. We want to validate that what they are feeling makes sense to us, that we also experience painful or difficult feelings, and that when they expose their pain in the therapy process they will not be quickly judged as a problem to be solved or seen as a burden or a threat, but rather will be joined in an experience of compassion. I like to tell clients that we are all entitled to our struggles in life. Struggling is part of what makes us human, and it offers us the opportunity to learn, grow and develop wisdom.

CONCLUSIONS

When we provide a new kind of relational home for our clients, we are reinforcing that they can be loved and accepted as they are. This does not mean that we would not help them manage their feelings in interpersonal interactions in ways that work for them or help them achieve their goals. But, in doing so, we do not question the feelings themselves or make their feelings wrong. If we are successful, our clients stand a much better chance of using the psychotherapy relationship as a model for how other intimate relationships in their lives can succeed, without requiring that they hide who they are from the people close to them.

THE COMPASSIONATE ENCOUNTER WITH THE SELF

To thine own self be true.
—WILLIAM SHAKESPEARE
Hamlet

SHINING OUR LIGHT ON OUR DARKNESS

In my years as a psychotherapist, I have increasingly come to believe that we don't find more light in our lives by trying to eliminate what feels dark, even though that often seems like the reasonable thing to do. Instead, it is by shining our light on our darkness that we become free to truly know ourselves and to accept and embrace the fullness of who we are. While this may require courage, it also leaves us stronger, since we learn to face and ultimately integrate that which previously felt dangerous or alien.

This process of bringing light to our darkness is what we encourage many of our clients to do in psychotherapy, particularly those who tend to avoid or compensate for their pain or vulnerability, leaving them out of touch with aspects of who they are. It illustrates the dimension of our work that is the most counterintuitive; rather than attempting to eliminate what feels dark in our lives, we purposely seek out that darkness and look directly at it. In doing so, we have the ability to reclaim aspects of ourselves that have been ignored, exiled or shamed.

An "encounter with the self" is not just an encounter with the parts of the self that we feel comfortable with, but an encounter with the unknown, unexpressed, or banished aspects as well. Therapists often refer to these unacknowledged parts as the "not me." Maybe the encounter is with something we dislike about ourselves. Or maybe it involves tapping into deeper emotions that we felt lurking down there but were not willing to expose before. The client may encounter a more vulnerable self, possibly what we refer to as the "inner child" that had been wounded, but whose deepest feelings have long since been covered over.

WHY THE JOURNEY IS WORTHWHILE

Why would anyone want to embark on this kind of journey when it feels more natural to sweep all the unpleasant thoughts and feelings under the rug and just move on with our lives? The answer is that psychotherapy is not a kind of torture where we dredge up old wounds, acknowledge our frailty and vulnerability, bring out the deepest levels of our pain and just suffer with it and let it fester. Quite the contrary; we are bringing our light to the darkness. Bringing our light to the darkness is not just a metaphor for *looking at* our darkness; we are talking about much more than just neutrally examining what is there. This is where compassion comes in.

When we as clients are able to own and acknowledge that which had previously been exiled, it is as if we are reunited with parts of ourselves that had been lost. In the presence of an empathic and accepting therapist, the client and the therapist together can bring loving compassion to just those parts that appear to get in the way the most or that seem the most frightening. The banished or neglected parts are now given a home, and by admitting to and expressing these thoughts and feelings, we are in fact *embracing* that part of the self that had previously been banished.

It often happens that finding a place of belonging for that wounded, suffering or vulnerable part of ourselves naturally brings forth feelings of loving compassion, and both clients and therapists share in the power and tenderness of these moments. When we take the risk to speak from a deeper place within us, the pain or sadness that is revealed can be transformed in the presence of the love that is released, and what had felt frightening or dark or heavy turns to relief and a sense of comfort. The tears and sadness may still be there, but the experience feels safe and loving.

I want to emphasize that it is not just accepting ourselves, but embracing ourselves. It is a homecoming. I believe that, for many of us, undertaking some version of this type of encounter with the self is ultimately what gives us access to our light and opens up the possibility for finding the most happiness and joy. But the process of exposing our vulnerability in safe circumstances is not a one-time occurrence. We continue in therapy to allow these "not me" parts to find expression. And long after our psychotherapy experience is over, life gives us many opportunities to successfully integrate this "not me" into our lives in ways that make us both happier and stronger.

THE PRICE OF AVOIDANCE

In some respects, it is a luxury to go to therapy and have a therapist serving as a compassionate guide, helping us to orchestrate a loving encounter with ourselves. Yet the choice to embark upon this journey is not an easy one. Encountering the self feels frightening; it is human nature to attempt to disown those parts of ourselves that hold our vulnerability, that feel too emotional, or the parts that are not "winning" in the world.

So rather than face them, we avoid them. We keep busy and compensate for our pain, longings or feelings of inadequacy by being even more successful in our careers, our athletic prowess, our accumulation of wealth, or in whatever ways work for us. Often we can get by, at least most of the time. If we manage our lives so that we have more successes than failures, we can feel somewhat protected. When we occasionally stumble, we nurse our wounds, push the unpleasant experience out of our awareness, and go back to feeling OK about ourselves.

After all, avoidance and compensation are often healthy defenses and are there for a reason. As we say to our clients, our defensive systems serve an important purpose; we have needed them, particularly when we were young, just to help us survive and feel strong and cohesive. But as we get older, these same defenses that worked so well in our lives can sometimes become counterproductive. While our coping strategies can work to some degree, they can also leave us with precarious self-esteem and can limit our ability to flourish. In the words of F. Forrester Church, former Minister of the Unitarian Church of All Souls in New York City:

So long as we don't think much about these things, letting life live us, burying our deepest feelings in sand running out unwatched through the funnel of our glass, this is tolerable. We insulate ourselves, build walls, block out the sun, rarely get burned. We aren't lost, not exactly, for we fit in a tight, if slightly uncomfortable frame. But we aren't saved either. We aren't even close to being saved.

Possibly what is most tragic about all of this is that our efforts to banish or ignore the wounded parts of ourselves often end up repeating the original damage. If we had a parent who was critical or shaming, for example, we end up shunning this same part of ourselves and trying to hide that "inadequate" or "defective" child from ourselves and from others, including our romantic partners. We may convince ourselves that our self-esteem is finally solid, only to be toppled over once again when our insecurities are exposed.

Or if a parent was cold or did not understand us, spend time with us, make us feel special or valued, or connect with us emotionally, then we may end up repeating the deprivation by ignoring our wounded or lonely child that was deprived in childhood. We might feel angry about our deprivation or, alternatively, we may deny that anything was wrong. But without the ability to face the pain of what we missed, we are clearly at a disadvantage when it comes to creating our own intimate relationships.

PRESENTING OUR FULL SELVES

For many people, love is not just the result of shared interests, mutual respect, or admiration for our strengths and successes. It is difficult to imagine a deep love that it not based, to some degree, on the ability to recognize and appreciate the most profound vulnerability of the other, and to respond to that vulnerability, at least on occasion, with so much compassion that it is felt by the other as a heartfelt embrace. If intimacy is defined as the ability to connect through our vulnerability, then the compassionate encounter with the self is often a necessary first step.

That same place that holds our pain, where our hearts have been broken, is often where we find our greatest sweetness and innocence. Ironically, it is often the parts of ourselves that we disapprove of or fear the most that turn out to be the most loveable and also the most capable of returning love. If we can reclaim our broken hearts, including all the sadness that is there, we are in a better position to create a healing experience of love in our lives. If we have come to know ourselves fully, we can show this formerly buried part of ourselves to our partners (or guide them to it). Without our help, how can they find us, love us and help us heal at this most profound level?

And if we have found compassion for our formerly exiled parts, we are much less likely to make what can be tragic mistakes in relationships. Rather than act out our disowned feelings or insecurities in some unconscious or inappropriate way, we can introduce these exiled parts of ourselves to our partners—not as something monstrous, but rather as aspects of ourselves that may need some healing, but that are ultimately worthy of love. While there is never any guarantee that our partners will accept all that we are, we are in a much better position to find a partner who truly loves us when we are conscious of and at least somewhat accepting of our full selves.

HELPING CLIENTS FIND SELF-COMPASSION

In looking at the role of compassion in psychotherapy, it is important to clarify that our intention as therapists is not to help a client to be a kinder or more compassionate person in the sense of how they relate to the world. But one thing that we generally do want to accomplish is to help clients find more self-compassion. The process of psychotherapy is well suited for this challenge, since we ask clients to open up and express parts of themselves that they normally do not reveal. And if we as therapists are successful in maintaining a compassionate and welcoming stance, our clients are more inclined, over time, to learn to do the same for themselves.

Yet most clients do not mention self-compassion as a goal, and some question whether having greater compassion for oneself is even a good thing. While everyone would like to have improved self-esteem, or to find a way to think more highly of themselves, the notion of having compassion for oneself is somewhat more complex. Some people react to the idea of compassion or forgiveness toward oneself in a negative way, as if there were something self-indulgent about it. (This word "self-indulgent" is frequently heard as a criticism of psychotherapy in general.) I often have clients tell me that they do not want to end up like the Stuart Smalley character on Saturday Night Live who looks into the mirror and repeats positive affirmations.

It is easy to make fun of Stuart Smalley's version of "self-acceptance," but as clients begin to understand what self-compassion actually entails, many come to see it in the opposite way, not as a cop-out or as something pathetic, but as a life journey that requires considerable courage and that helps us to be stronger, not weaker. With greater self-exploration and compassion for what we discover, we stand more solidly grounded in the full truth of who we are and can better tap the potentials inherent in our more complete selves. And having compassion for ourselves does not mean that we avoid making changes or taking risks. Quite the contrary, we are less likely to make healthy changes and move forward if we are hiding from or not acknowledging essential aspects of ourselves or our emotional life, or if we are weighed down by criticisms of ourselves or what we consider our failings.

THE POTENTIAL FOR TRANSFORMATION

...To make it through life without conspicuous incident is not enough. Life's goal is not to live safely, not even to live forever. It is to live fully, even to die before we die, that we may be reborn, recast, refired in the furnace of pain, hope and possibility.

—F. FORRESTER CHURCH

COMPASSION, TRANSCENDENCE AND TRANSFORMATION

Why is compassion considered to be a spiritual emotion, as opposed to other related concepts such as "empathy," "sympathy" or "altruism"? What is there about compassion that elevates it to the spiritual plane? The answer is that compassion has something basic in common with other words that we associate with spirituality, including "love," "beauty" and "awe." What ultimately unites these words is that they all convey a sense of transcendence. Whether we are the giver or the receiver, the experience of compassion has the power to take us beyond our ordinary limits. We achieve a special connection or sense of belonging that can transcend our normal ego-driven concerns.

Transformation is another word to describe what can happen when vulnerability or grief is exposed and met with compassion. What was suffering, sadness or fear can shift to a feeling of relief or release, which can be quite dramatic or can also be more subtle. But either way, both people generally experience it together. In that moment, both are transformed.

There is a longer-term transformation as well. Psychotherapy gives us an opportunity to challenge the safe life, to "die before we die" in order to be "reborn." When we humble ourselves enough in psychotherapy to allow banished parts to emerge, we challenge the whole of our being. We offer ourselves the ultimate healing, but in doing so our old selves must die in a way. When we expose and explore our deepest thoughts and feelings, we change who we are.

What is most noteworthy about the Forrest Church quote is that it inspires us to want to take that leap and enter the furnace. His words connect us with a deep longing to be reborn and to live fully. We know instinctively that exposing ourselves to that furnace and the pain that goes with it is essential to our mission. Like clay that has not yet been molded to show its true beauty, we yearn to achieve our potential—to be "reborn, recast, refired in the furnace of pain, hope and possibility."

PARALLELS WITH RELIGION AND SPIRITUALITY

While these dynamics play an important role in psychotherapy, it is clear that the miracle that I am calling transformation or transcendence through the experience of loving compassion was not just invented or discovered by psychotherapists. It is more accurate to say that what makes these dynamics so effective in psychotherapy is that we have created a structure that is well-suited to facilitating basic human emotional processes that have been with mankind for many centuries and are related, I believe, to religious experiences of feeling redeemed or saved. What in psychotherapy we call transformation might be called salvation or redemption in a religious context.

Of course, these words do not describe exactly the same thing. But the themes of religious salvation and psychological transformation are parallel in the sense that salvation is about being forgiven and finding a home with a merciful God, while in psychotherapy we work with a therapist to find a compassionate and forgiving home for ourselves. In today's world, psychotherapy is one of the few institutions (along with what is offered in twelve step programs and in certain religious or spiritual communities) where we are encouraged to let go of control enough to experience the kind of shift that might be called transcendent or transformational.

I introduce here some poetic words from the world of religion or spirituality that may help bring to life this experience of transformation and also highlight some of the parallels between the experience of loving compassion in psychotherapy and in spirituality.

AMAZING GRACE THAT CAN SAVE OUR SOULS

Sometimes the best way to find truth is not to read the philosophers, the academics or the religious theory, but to look at the words of the songs that have withstood the test of time and speak directly to the human condition. Being popular doesn't make it ordinary; it proves that it is powerful. In the case of "Amazing Grace," what it means to us undoubtedly has changed from its original meaning in the 1700s when the words were first written. In those days "grace" probably referred to religious salvation—something bestowed directly from a merciful God who could forgive us, redeem our sins, and save our souls from eternal damnation.

Amazing grace! How sweet the sound
that saved a wretch like me.
I once was lost, but now am found,
was blind but now I see.

After undergoing a period of obscurity, the hymn re-emerged, and those same words now speak to us once again. Contemporary man still responds to the concept of salvation. At some visceral level, most people relate to an experience of grace. Not just a subtle grace, but a magnificent and amazing grace that is sweet, loving, compassionate and forgiving, a grace that is so amazing that it can save us. It may not save us from eternal damnation in a fire and brimstone hell, but it can save us from alienation and from other modern versions of damnation.

It is the ultimate transformation, from being lost to being found, from being blind to seeing. And since we can believe in grace without believing in a personal or omniscient God, it doesn't require a deity to make it real. Ultimately it is about mercy, the human emotional experience, and the ability of loving compassion to provide a home for us.

A number of years ago there were attempts to remove the word "wretch" from "Amazing Grace" and substitute something more benign, such as "saved a soul like me" or "saved and strengthened me." But many objected, and it now appears that the public has voted and the word "wretch" has been reinstated. I believe that this is as it should be. If we acknowledge that we are wretched, that we are lost or that we are blind, this humbled position may be the best vantage point for finding grace.

THE "SISTERS OF MERCY" ARE WAITING FOR US

What better way to be reminded of the possibility of grace than Leonard Cohen's beautiful song "Sisters of Mercy." His words help bridge the gap between a religious understanding of salvation through grace and a more psychological understanding of transformation through the power of loving compassion. The narrator is letting us know that there is hope: the Sisters of Mercy are not departed, they are not gone; they are waiting to help us when we really need them. He has proof, since in his time of darkness, when he felt that he just could not go on, when he was brought to his knees, they were there.

Oh, the Sisters of Mercy
They are not departed or gone
They were waiting for me
When I thought that I just can't go on
And they brought me their comfort
And later they brought me their song
Oh, I hope you run into them
You who've been traveling so long.

—LEONARD COHEN
Excerpt from "Sisters of Mercy"

There is a religious theme throughout this song, although the metaphor is not about a God figure, but rather about "sisters." It brings to mind the image of merciful nuns in flowing robes, the kind that are humbly dedicated to those whom the rest of the world are most inclined to neglect. This is not the symbolism of a powerful male God who saves our souls from sin and offers redemption in exchange for belief or commitment, but rather these lovely sisters who offer mercy, kindness and comfort with no strings attached.

COMPASSION AS THE PATH FROM ALIENATION TO BELONGING

In the second verse the topic of sin is introduced, but not sin in the religious sense of specific indiscretions that need to be confessed. The sin in this song is about the psychological position of contemporary man and our efforts to control. Once we establish this pattern of needing to control, we are in danger of losing our souls. Our souls must be free to live and breathe; we need the full aliveness of our souls, since it is that aliveness that helps us to recognize our souls in the first place.

The song states that when we are "not feeling holy," it is our "loneliness" that tells us that we have sinned. I believe that another way to describe the loneliness is alienation. The narrator is released from his loneliness and alienation when the sisters lie down beside him and he makes his "confession" to them. The sisters bring a compassionate love that overcomes the alienation. They offer a "graceful" and "binding" love that reconnects us to life, just as a leaf that has been torn off and blown about by the seasons once again finds a stem. What had been an experience of alienation is transformed to an experience of belonging.

The narrator implies that this is not really his song. Rather, the sisters brought it to him, and, in his gratitude, he wishes to share it with us. He knows that we, too, have been traveling for a very long time. Unlike the possessiveness that we associate with sexual or romantic love, he would not be jealous if the sisters "sweeten" our night. While there is touching involved, it is not in a sexual way. This is a different kind of love, and there is plenty to go around.

WE MUST SEEK IN ORDER TO FIND

Ask, and it will be given to you; seek, and you will find; knock, and it will be opened to you.

—MATTHEW 7:7

You will seek me and find me when you seek me with all your heart.

—JEREMIAH 29:13

It makes sense that we need to first seek in order to find. If we are doing OK and going about our normal lives, we are not open to dying and being reborn. But when we are lost or wretched, that is the time when we might risk the encounter with the self. We need to be in touch with our suffering or our vulnerability if we are to experience grace or "run into" the Sisters of Mercy. I like the phrase "brought to our knees." I often tell clients that it can be surprising to see what comes once we are truly "brought to our knees."

Psychotherapy offers a contemporary version of seeking. Just the gesture of going to therapy implies that we are relinquishing a certain amount of control and are admitting that we cannot solve our problems on our own. We must go in and face another person and, in effect, make our "confession" and explain our problems and challenges. We open up and speak honestly about our lives, our fears, our hopes, our joys, our pain and our failures. We need the courage to confess, to acknowledge our powerlessness and to seek with an open heart.

And in our confessional mode we sometimes find, often to our surprise, that the Sisters of Mercy are waiting for us. Even though psychotherapy has nothing to do with forgiveness of sins by a merciful God, most therapists would agree that, in our work, we witness many moments of what could be called "grace." But it would be wrong to suggest that psychotherapists represent the Sisters of Mercy. Psychotherapists are facilitators for the power of loving compassion, and this is what "Sisters of Mercy" represents.

THE SOUL JOURNEY: REFRAMING THE MEANING OF SUFFERING

In describing the transformational potential of compassion, I do not mean to give the impression that we as therapists can always help clients achieve emotional shifts that can transform their suffering through something that feels like "amazing grace." The words of the Buddha celebrate the *potential* of compassion to "crush" and "destroy" the pain of those who suffer. But this is certainly not always the case, and, when it does happen, it cannot be expected to occur in every session.

Much of the time in psychotherapy the best that we can do is to stay present with our clients in their times of suffering and offer them companionship and human connection. We do this by joining with them rather than reassuring them that things are not really so bad or trying to help them see their position in a more positive light. Trying to convince someone that their fears or concerns are exaggerated can be helpful at times, but this is not the gesture of joining. Cognitive therapy is based upon challenging negative thoughts that are distorted, and this can be useful, but healing through compassion takes a different form.

THE AWFUL GRACE OF GOD

I would like to illustrate the power of joining with suffering by referencing a now famous speech by Robert Kennedy that was given to a largely black audience in Indianapolis. Kennedy had found out just prior to the speech that Martin Luther King had been shot. As Kennedy spoke to the unknowing audience, he announced the tragic news. In *Politics Lost*, Joe Klein describes the screams and wailing that ensued—"just the rawest, most visceral sounds of pain that human voices can summon." After the screaming subsided, Kennedy addressed them, "laying himself bare," and spoke of his brother's death. Kennedy then recited from his favorite poem, referenced below, by the poet Aeschylus. The moment, as Klein described it, was "stunning."

Even in our sleep, pain which cannot forget
falls drop by drop upon the heart...
until... in our own despair, against our will,
comes wisdom through the awful grace of God.
—AESCHYLUS
As quoted by Robert Kennedy

Apparently Robert Kennedy knew the kind of despair when, against our will and through our pain, we receive wisdom through the awful grace of God. He had to come to terms with the death of his brother, as well as with whatever other hardships and challenges he faced in his life. Kennedy's willingness to share these very private thoughts with his audience made it possible for everyone to grieve together. His words are a reminder that suffering can unite us; in fact, our human suffering may be the essence of what unites us or ties us together at the deepest level. Maybe that is why pain and suffering can be associated with "grace," even though it can be an "awful grace."

REMEMBERING THAT LIFE IS DIFFICULT

One of the plagues of our modern culture is that we tend to forget that life is not designed for happiness and, in fact, a certain amount of difficulty and suffering is normal and to be expected. Our ancestors probably understood this all too well, since there was no way to avoid being face to face with the suffering of humanity; the realities of death, illness, starvation, war, poverty, and mental and emotional anguish were more out front for all to witness. Today we are able to insulate ourselves from much of the pain of our neighbors and instead rely on sources such as television or other media to inform us of how our fellow humans are coping, leading many to conclude that other people are mostly happy, that we are somehow alone in our suffering.

Fortunately the world of spirituality offers plenty of poetic language that tells us otherwise and serves to remind us of our human condition. Even though we often associate spirituality with feeling uplifted and hopeful, there is also a major dimension of the spiritual literature that speaks directly to the suffering side of life. In fact, the human struggle has a special meaning in the spiritual lexicon. Spiritual writers have always taken a particular interest in re-framing human suffering, thereby giving it a context or a meaning so that we are more able to accept it and, at times, embrace it. This is the language that can meet us and speak to us when we are doubting, struggling, lost, or otherwise feeling like we have failed.

ALLOWING YOURSELF TO BE LOST

I have found in my practice that it is this literature of darkness and struggle that is often the most comforting and reassuring. What I find most helpful with clients is to remind them not only that life is difficult and that they need not feel alone or alienated in painful times, but that they deserve respect as well. We are each embarking on our own unique quest for meaning, purpose and fulfillment. If we are committed to using our own experience to guide us, then we cannot rely on pre-established formulas or cultural prototypes to determine the path that we will follow. But it takes considerable courage to take the journey our own way, and we must expect that sometimes we will be lost.

As we go about creating our own maps that identify our goals and how to get there, we become wedded to these templates that we have constructed. Unfortunately the process does not seem to be about incrementally building one map throughout one's lifetime. Rather, we often need to discard or at least seriously revise some of the maps that had previously provided us with much of our vision, philosophy and, to some extent, our identities. When an old map is not working, that experience is hard to deny. So we find ourselves in a transitional state, needing to discard an old map and not able to envision a new one. Yet in this confusion often lies great opportunity.

Contemporary American poet David Whyte sums this up as "the wisdom of allowing yourself to be lost in the world." He says something that I have repeated many times to my clients and that never fails to produce a positive shift or a pleasantly surprised response. He says that if you can see the path ahead of you, then it is not your path. You can tell if it is your path because it disappears. Anthropologist Joseph Campbell speaks eloquently about the heroism of the human journey and the wisdom of being lost:

If you can see your path laid out in front of you step by step, you know it's not your path. Your own path you make with every step you take. That's why it's your path.

THE HEROIC ASPECT OF SUFFERING

What do therapists do when our clients are feeling despairing or discouraged, or when they are comparing themselves unfavorably to friends or to other people? Often these are not moments to remind them of their successes or to make suggestions for how they can get unstuck and move forward. But in these moments we do have some options available other than just appearing to give in to their despair.

I have found that, when clients are in this despairing place, I can always remind them that they are indeed heroes of their own journeys, and that ultimately their journeys cannot be compared with those of anyone else. We all have ebbs and flows in our lives and are entitled to our pain and to pursue our process in the best way that we can. I like to think that we are comparable to the heroes in the ancient myths; we also encounter demons along our paths, and we are forced to take on these demons and hope that we will develop wisdom as a result. Yet there is no guarantee of the outcome or whether our journey will feel like a success in the end.

This is heroic and our clients deserve to recognize this. By calling our journeys "heroic," we are no longer critical or shaming of ourselves, and we are no longer feeling alienated. Instead, we bring in compassion and respect. And even if I don't say this out loud, it helps me tremendously as a therapist to witness the heroism of my clients and to respond to them accordingly.

THE MESSAGE OF EASTER

On Easter Sunday of 1993 I attended a sermon at the All Souls Unitarian Church in New York City given by minister Forrest Church. At the time I was just beginning my work as a therapist, and although I had not yet formulated my ideas about compassion, I knew that the sermon carried a very profound message, and I have kept the hard copy ever since. It had been lost among my books and papers for many years, but fortunately I was able to recover it twenty years later.

What was most striking about the sermon was something that I will always remember—the way the minister described Jesus. It was not just that Jesus suffered and died on the cross, but that Jesus is also "a failure." As the minister Forrest Church put it, "His disciples believed that he would march into Jerusalem and ascend to David's rightful throne, as scion and messiah. Instead, he was betrayed and crucified." Later he adds, "Jesus failed more monumentally than any of us will ever fail. Just when he thought he had put it all together, he was betrayed, killed, and forsaken by those who loved him. It doesn't get any worse than that."

Yet now, two thousand years later, we celebrate this tragic experience and proclaim Jesus to be the son of God. Forrest Church did not believe that Jesus was "the Christ" or at least not "the only Christ," nor did he believe that Jesus was resurrected from the dead in a literal sense. But he did believe that Jesus was a savior, not a savior in the sense that we are saved by believing in him, but rather in the sense of what Jesus taught:

> *His cross is more lofty than any throne, because the final defeat is a victory, a victory of forgiveness over judgment and love over fear.*

JOY AND GRATITUDE

JOY AS A SPIRITUAL EMOTION

Joy descends gently upon us like the evening dew, and does not patter down like a hailstorm.
—JEAN PAUL F. RICHTER

Joy is not the absence of suffering. It is the presence of God.
—ROBERT SCHULLER

JOY VERSUS HAPPINESS

Happiness can occur at any point in our lives, but finding joy often takes a lifetime. Joy is not guaranteed; it seems to be something that we must earn after we struggle with life's challenges and emerge stronger and wiser as a result. But once we have really found joy, it claims a permanent place within us. Even though we cannot always access it, joy does not desert us; unlike happiness, which is fleeting, joy is associated with words like "abiding," "everlasting" and "immutable."

Even though I am uncomfortable with the word "God," I chose to highlight the Robert Schuller quote because he makes his point so beautifully and so simply. We do not need to believe in a personal God to understand what he means when he says that joy is not the absence of suffering but the presence of God. It is difficult to imagine happiness coinciding with suffering, yet joy operates on a different plane than our personal ups and downs. Joy seems to come from a deeper place within us that is less dependent upon circumstances and more about our overall outlook—how we experience ourselves and the world around us. We can go through our phases of happiness and suffering and still know a pure joy that is simmering beneath the surface.

JOY CAN BE SUBTLE

Most of us know intuitively that there is something "spiritual" about joy, that it deserves to be classified as a spiritual emotion, while happiness does not. Like love, joy has a transcendent quality that takes us beyond the normal boundaries of our individual personalities and connects us with something that feels all encompassing. We associate joy with intense emotional states such as "bliss," "euphoria," "ecstasy," "exultation" and "rapture," but joy can also present itself in a much quieter, subtle way that feels more like a sense of peace or well-being.

When I think of joy I often imagine Buddhist monks who are able to transform themselves and become "enlightened" after spending years at the monastery in silent meditation and study. Yet, for many of us, joy is within our reach, even if we have failed to obtain full enlightenment. Our experience of joy does not have to be dramatic or blissful; we can consider ourselves blessed if we can relate to the above quote; joy does not need to come down like a hailstorm. Most of us will be more than content to have joy descend gently upon us in our later years, like the evening dew.

THE RELATIONSHIP BETWEEN JOY AND GRATITUDE

We hold the key to lasting happiness in our own hands.
For it is not joy that makes us grateful; it is gratitude
that makes us joyful.

—BROTHER DAVID STEINDL-RAST
Gratefulness, the Heart of Prayer

Brother David Steindl-Rast believes that we often misunderstand the role that gratitude plays in our lives. Rather than being an offshoot of joy, he claims that gratitude is at the root of joy. First we find gratitude, and then we find joy, not the other way around. Thinking of joy and gratitude in this way helps to clarify what joy really stands for and why joy does not depend upon good fortune, material success, or even good health.

Gratitude is not a function of the tangible ways that life has rewarded us—for example, with money, fame, security, status, comfort, the freedom to travel, and so on. Gratitude is more about the nature of our relationship to life in general than it is about the kind of luck we have or what we possess. There is absolutely nothing wrong with aspiring to all of these things, and they can certainly make us happy for awhile, but they do not hold the key to joy. We all know people who are grateful and possess very little or have had bad luck in life. And we know people who have succeeded in all the material ways and still the sense of gratitude (and therefore joy) eludes them.

COMING BACK TO THE PRESENT MOMENT

To understand joy and gratitude, we come back to the importance of knowing how to be present. We find ourselves back to "the now," the same place where we started when discussing awe. It is not surprising that an exploration of the spiritual emotions takes us back to the beginning; after all, the spiritual emotions can never really be separated. While it is true that awe, faith, love, compassion, joy and gratitude highlight different dynamics or different qualities, the feelings that we are describing all ultimately go together.

When we discussed awe, we were emphasizing the wonder of finding the "more" in the moment, as well as the adventure of discovering our own version of felt meaning. Being in the moment is also the key to gratitude, but it is a different kind of "more" in the moment. With gratitude we are speaking about "accepting what is." This is not a resigned acceptance; it is an active appreciation. Our gratefulness in the moment is an experience of fullness, the "Great Fullness," as Brother David says.

When the moment does not feel full, it is only natural to want something more. Most of us probably feel this desire for something more much of the time. Finding lasting joy does not mean that we always feel grateful; it means that we know the fullness in the moment, and that we can periodically return to that place, if only on occasion. As humans, we are inclined to feel in competition with the rest of the world for what we need, and this is certainly true from the standpoint of basic survival, so a conscious effort may be required to set aside the time and space to make room for gratitude.

FOCUS ON WHAT YOU FEEL GRATEFUL FOR

Is it possible that we really do hold the key to lasting happiness in our own hands? If we set a goal to find more joy in our lives, it is not clear exactly how we would begin. But having gratitude as a goal offers a certain clarity of purpose. Brother David believes that there are simple things that we can do to deepen our gratefulness and, as a result, move closer to joy. His suggestion: take the time to focus on what you are grateful for. We know what has contributed to feelings of gratitude in the past, and we need to remember this, learn from our experience, and consciously bring more gratitude into our lives. This advice is so simple, but not always easy to follow.

Scientific research increasingly confirms this view. While poverty is detrimental to happiness, once a basic level of safety or comfort is achieved, having more wealth or more success is not correlated with greater happiness. Interestingly, in searching for behaviors that promote happiness, a major study reported that there was one activity that stood out well above the rest. What created the most happiness for the people in the study was when they were told to seek out important people in their lives and directly express their gratitude to them. I imagine that most of us can think of people who might be quite surprised and touched to hear how profoundly they have influenced us and how much they mean to us. It is easy to imagine feeling joyful when we can overcome our reluctance or our shyness and directly share our sentiments of gratitude.

FINDING GRATITUDE LATER IN LIFE

Old age has its obvious shortcomings, but when it comes to

experiencing gratitude, there are some real advantages to being near the end of life. First, there is less pressure to create the right future for oneself; that job, for the most part, has been completed, for better or for worse. So being present in the "now" becomes a more natural place to reside. And this is particularly true when the many opportunities to distract ourselves from the present moment have lost some of their charm.

But the real edge comes when the prospect of one's own death ceases to be an abstraction and becomes a reality. It is easier to feel grateful, I believe, if we can actually see death right over our shoulder. In the beginning of our lives, as children and adolescents, we are discovering life freshly, trying to make sense of it, and attempting to find our place in it. But as we approach our death, we begin to say goodbye to life and to all that we have found meaningful. And, in saying goodbye, everything takes on a different quality. Life becomes more "poignant."

I illustrate this with a scene from the science fiction movie Blade Runner—an unlikely source for a book about the poetry of spirituality, but I include it here because it is considered by some to be the most moving death soliloquy in cinematic history. Blade Runner tells the tale of a series of man-made "replicants" who have become aware that their relatively short lives are soon programmed to end. Like humans, they have developed the desire to prolong their lives, but ultimately they are defeated when the last remaining replicant, Roy, who is the most intelligent and also the most violent, discovers that the scientific genius who created him does not have the power to reverse his programming. In the now famous ending monologue, Roy withdraws from attacking the police officer who seeks to apprehend him and speaks tearfully in a rain storm, right before he dies.

I've seen things you people wouldn't believe... Attack ships on fire off the shoulder of Orion. I watched C-beams glitter in the dark near the Tannhauser Gate. All those... moments... will be lost in time, like tears in rain. Time... to... die.

As he talks, we watch Roy transition from a ruthless killer to a gentler being who sadly recalls the magnificence of what he has witnessed in his short life. It is both tragic and profoundly moving to think that we and all that has been meaningful to us, our version of the C-beams glittering in the dark near the Tannhauser gate, will soon be lost in time. We hope to make a difference, to leave our mark on the universe, but ultimately we are like "tears in rain."

The beauty of our world is magnified by the tragic awareness that we are about to lose it. When life feels poignant in this way, it is easier to feel grateful. We see more clearly the preciousness of all that we will leave behind. Thus, for many people, there is the irony of feeling more grateful (and therefore more joyful) at the same time that life feels the most precarious.

HEEDING THE SOUL'S CALLING

Joy, rather than happiness, is the goal of life, for joy is the emotion which accompanies our fulfilling our natures as human beings.

—ROLLO MAY
Man's Search for Himself

What I know for sure is that you feel joy in direct proportion to how connected you are to living your truth.

—OPRAH WINFREY
O Magazine, May 2001

The literature and poetry on the topic of joy make frequent references to the concept of the soul. Joy, gratitude and soul all seem to be related, but each reflects a different vantage point. Joy is more like an emotion; gratitude is a combination of an emotion and an attitude—a way of experiencing our relationship to the world; but soul is neither an emotion nor an attitude. It is a metaphor for an aspect of our being, something that permanently resides within us. Our souls reflect our uniqueness, our essence and our deepest longings. They grow and develop as we grow, but, paradoxically, they also transcend our individual personalities and connect us with something expansive.

Finding more gratitude is one way to conceptualize the path

to joy. Another way is to look to our souls. For those who relate to the word "soul," it makes sense that the soul would have to be involved in order to experience joy. Joy implies an engagement at the deepest level of who we are. If our souls represent the core of us, then by finding and developing our souls we can come closer to our core and closer to finding joy. If we are living our lives in such as way that our personalities and our souls are in alignment, then we are opening the door to the possibility of joy.

BELIEVING IN OUR SOULS

That luminous part of you that exists beyond personality—your soul, if you will—is as bright and shining as any that has ever been. Bright as Shakespeare's; bright as Ghandi's, bright as Mother Teresa's. Clear away everything that keeps you separate from this secret, luminous place. Believe it exists, come to know it better, nurture it, share its fruits tirelessly.
—GEORGE SAUNDERS
The Convocation Speech at Syracuse University (2013)

The concept of soul is something that, by its very nature, defies definition. Yet George Saunders' words capture the essence of what we mean by the "soul" in a way that our souls can actually recognize and respond to. In his speech to the graduates of Syracuse University he calls out to our souls and proclaims their great value. We need not be modest; our souls are not lesser just because we have failed to obtain worldwide recognition as great spiritual leaders or literary geniuses. He helps us to recognize that, yes, it makes sense that our soul is "as bright and shining as any that has ever been."

I am trying to imagine how I would have felt as a young student being given this advice upon graduation. I think my response would have been some combination of surprise, confusion and excitement. This is not the typical rallying call of a commencement address; that moment is usually reserved for some type of invitation to go into the world, have confidence in ourselves, and fight the good fight. I remember being told that with hard work and perseverance we can accomplish what we want in the world—more like a coach getting their team ready for battle.

Saunders tells the students to focus on something quite different; his speech emphasizes the importance of kindness as opposed to accomplishment. And he reminds us that the soul is truly a paradoxical concept. On the one hand, it is bright, shining and luminous, and yet it is also shy and easy to dismiss, a secret place. That same place within us that can shine in such a recognizable way is also strangely elusive. Not surprisingly, our rational minds have trouble believing in and processing what exists at the soul level. Saunders encourages us to believe that our souls exist and to make a point of nurturing them and prioritizing them in our lives.

FINDING YOUR SOUL PATH

So much of our challenge in life is about forging our own unique path and finding the work, vocation or way of expressing ourselves in the world that feels true to our inner-being—a path that reflects who we are at the level of the heart and the soul. Not everyone would be expected to feel a calling in this way, but for those who do, the search can be a difficult one. As the saying goes, "Many are called, but few are chosen." Having a vague sense of personal calling is one thing, but really listening to it, understanding it, prioritizing it and then successfully manifesting it in the world is a tall order.

How do we find a way to live that enables our entire beings—including heart, mind and soul—to flourish? The first step, as George Saunders tells the students in his commencement speech, is to "clear away everything that keeps you separate from this secret, luminous place" that is the soul. He makes it sound easy, but of course this can be a life's work, in and of itself. And once we learn to access our soul, we must "believe it exists, come to know it better, nurture it, and share it's fruits tirelessly."

Maybe the best way to think about the search for our soul path is to see it as a process that has value in and of itself, regardless of the outcome. We can feel grateful just to be engaged in the quest to find and manifest our personal calling. It is a noble quest, whether or not we ever completely succeed or finish the journey. Fortunately there are many poetic sources from the literature of spirituality that can guide us and remind us to listen to that sometimes quiet voice within that may ultimately hold the answers and point the way to the soul path that we long to find.

THE POETRY OF PERSONAL CALLING

Before you tell your life what you intend to do with it, let your life tell you what truths you embody, what values you represent.

—PARKER J. PALMER
Let Your Life Speak: Listening for the Voice of Vocation

Our deepest calling is to grow into our own authentic selfhood, whether or not it conforms to some image of who we ought to be. As we do so, we will not only find the joy that every human being seeks—we will also find our path of authentic service in the world.
—PARKER J. PALMER
Let Your Life Speak: Listening for the Voice of Vocation

The most basic truth that comes from the literature on personal calling is that we must first learn to listen to ourselves—and this listening is often at a deeper level than what we are accustomed to and may take many years to accomplish. "Letting our life speak" is quite different from what our rational minds might want for us. It feels counterintuitive to bypass our more willful self and instead take the more humble position of listening. This kind of listening requires discipline and considerable patience—not something we tend to associate with vocational decision making. We must learn to listen in a way that our souls can respond to; as Palmer says, "the soul speaks its truth only under quiet, inviting, and trustworthy conditions."

The literature on personal calling also introduces the possibility of a wonderful kind of synchronicity—that when we are acting from our place of truth in the world we are doing much more than just gratifying ourselves; we are also serving the world in a special way. Isn't it a far greater achievement to find and act from our most authentic selves than to try to be or do something that does not truly resonate for us? I like to think that the world needs our deeply authentic contribution more than anything else that we might offer, no matter how noble or impressive those other strivings may appear to be.

JOINING THE GREAT SONG

When our hearts, minds and souls are in alignment and we are expressing ourselves in the world in a way that feels fulfilling, we are accomplishing a great deal. On one level we are offering the world what is uniquely ours at our best— something that combines our personal strengths and passions. But at another level we also enter the realm of the spiritual. Even though our callings reflect our individual personalities, the involvement of our souls ensures that we also transcend the personal, that we join with something greater. I illustrate this with my very favorite of all the spiritual poetry.

There is only one song, and it's the Great Song,
the Cosmic Song; it's the song that all things and
all animals and all plants and all humans sing
in their deepest heart.

And every song that a human being sings
with his or her voice is only an expression of that
one Great Song that is there from the beginning
and will be there after the end.

—BROTHER DAVID STEINDL-RAST
"Hymn to the Great Song"

It is difficult to imagine a greater achievement than being able to sing the Great Song. In doing so, we have the honor of joining with all the things, animals, plants and humans who are singing from their "deepest heart." Each of the participants offers their own unique voice, and yet all of these voices are ultimately an expression of that one Great and

Cosmic song which is eternal; "it is there from the beginning and will be there after the end."

When we are heeding our soul's calling, we are not feeling isolated, lost, alienated or afraid. Although we sometimes think of the world of vocation as a zero sum game that pits us against our competitors, fulfilling our soul's desire does just the opposite. It unites us with all of life in the ultimate experience of belonging. When we join with life in this way, joy and gratitude naturally follow.

We must ask ourselves a fundamental question: Have we accessed, prioritized and nurtured our souls sufficiently in our lives that we might have the opportunity to sing from our deepest heart and join in the Great Song? Or will we die with the music still inside us? Although our time is limited, it is never too late to begin. I include the following lines from a Bruce Carroll song that has helped to motivate and inspire me and may offer the same for you.

A wise man said most people die
With the music still inside of them
What a shame in a world
So in need of a song
As long as my heart has a rhythm
You're gonna hear from me again
I got a melody or two before I'm gone

—BRUCE CARROLL AND BILLY SPRAGUE
"Here I Go Again"

ABOUT THE AUTHOR

Elizabeth (Eli) Dickson, LCSW is a psychotherapist in private practice in New York City who is committed to integrating diverse approaches in her work. She received a Masters Degree in Social Work from New York University in 1995 and specializes in relationship issues, couples therapy and financial psychotherapy.

Eli's practice has been enriched by a prior career in economics and finance. After graduating from Smith College, she received a Masters in Public Policy from the University of California at Berkeley and went on to serve as Director of a Policy Analysis Division for New York City mayor Ed Koch, and later as a Bond Analyst at Smith Barney, where she was promoted to Vice-President.

She decided to become a psychotherapist for two reasons: She wanted to have an overview of the field of psychology and how people function, and she wanted the opportunity to connect at an emotional level, to be immersed in the more poetic, inspirational, heartfelt side of life.

WEBSITES BY ELI DICKSON

www.relationshiprealizations.com

www.psychotherapy-integration.com

www.soulofpsychotherapy.com

ACKNOWLEDGMENTS

Our own integrations of experience and insight are built on a foundation of other's integrations and insights, and soon our contribution will be swept into another's even more fruitful comprehension. We need each individual's integration. Each new viewpoint adds a facet. This presents us with the paradox of integration leading to diversity!

—LOUIS SANDER
Referenced by Lynn Preston and Ellen Shumsky in
"Toward an Integrative Sensibility"

I want to offer special thanks to my niece Mollie Dickson for her invaluable help in putting this book together and getting it out into the world. I also wish to thank my niece Rose Dickson for all the encouragement and ideas that came out of our collaboration on the picture version of this book, my brother David Dickson for believing in this project and keeping me going, my husband Tom Donovan for supporting me in a way that only a soulmate can, and Linda Levy for her coaching and suggestions. A major source of inspiration has been my mentor Lynn Preston, director of The Experiential Psychotherapy Project (EPP) in New York City, and through her influence, the philosophy of Eugene Gendlin, the founder of Focusing.

In tackling this huge project, I found that the only sure way to navigate through the complexity was to let myself be guided by the writings and poetry that moved me the most deeply. So I started there and let the concepts and ideas fall into place. Of the spiritual writers, most important have been the words of Brother David Steindl-Rast, a Benedictine monk who is both a poet and a philosopher—someone whose vision of spirituality is expressive and, at the same time, analytic and comprehensive. In addition, I have drawn inspiration from many other contemporary poet-philosophers, including but not limited to Pema Chodron, David Whyte, Jon Kabat-Zinn, and Rachel Naomi Remen. I am extremely grateful that life has given me the opportunity to attempt my own integration of such a compelling and elusive topic as spirituality and psychotherapy.

BIBLIOGRAPHY

Blade Runner. Directed by Ridley Scott. Warner Brothers, 1982. Film.

Buber, Martin. *Distance and Relation.* Translated by Ronald Gregor Smith. *The Hibbert Journal,* January 1951, Vol. XLIX, pp. 105-113.

Buber, Martin. *I and Thou.* New York: Charles Scribner's Sons, 1970.

Carroll, Bruce and Sprague, Billy. "Here I Go Again." *Speed of Light.* Nashville: Benson Music Group, 1996. CD. Copyright 1995 Word Music (a Div. of Word, Inc.)/ Skin Horse Music/ ASCAP.

Chodron, Pema. *Awakening Loving Kindness.* Boston: Shambhala, 1991.

Chodron, Pema. *When Things Fall Apart.* Boston: Shambhala, 1997.

Chodron, Pema. *Comfortable With Uncertainty.* Boston: Shambhala, 2002.

Church, Forrester F. "Part II: The Savior." *Three Faces of God: A Sermon Series.* The Unitarian Church of all Souls, New York City, April 1993.

Cohen, Leonard. "Sisters of Mercy." *The Best of Leonard Cohen.* New York: CBS Records, 1975. CD. Copyright 1967 Stranger Music, Inc. (BMI).

"Days pass and the years vanish. . ." from *Gates of Prayer: The New Union Prayer Book*. The Central Conference of American Rabbis.

Dante Alighieri. *The Comedy of Dante Alighieri, the Florentine*. Translated by Dorothy Sayers and Barbara Reynolds. Penguin Books, 1949.

Einstein, Albert. *The World As I See It*. Philosophical Library, 2011.

Fromm, Erich. *The Art of Loving*. New York: Harper & Row, 1956.

Gendlin, Eugene. *Focusing-Oriented Psychotherapy: A Manual of the Experiential Method*. New York: Guilford Press, 1996.

Heschel, Abraham Joshua. *Who Is Man?* Stanford University Press, 1965.

Hubble, Mark, Duncan, Barry and Miller, Scott. *The Heart and Soul of Change: What Works in Therapy*. Washington, D.C.: American Psychological Association, 1991.

Iadavaia, Angela (editor). *Common Sense Spirituality: The Essential Wisdom of David Steindl-Rast*. New York: Crossroad Publishing Company, 2008.

Kabat-Zinn, Jon. *Wherever You Go, There You Are*. New York: Hyperion, 1994.

Klein, Joe. "Prologue." *Politics Lost*. New York: Doubleday, 2006.

May, Rollo. *Man's Search for Himself*. New York: Norton, 1953.

Oliver, Mary. "Wild Geese." *Dream Work*. New York: Atlantic Monthly Press, 1986.

Orange, Donna. *Thinking for Clinicians*. New York: Routledge, 2010.

Palmer, Parker J. *Let your Life Speak: Listening for the Voice of Vocation*. San Francisco: John Wiley & Sons, 2000.

Preston, Lynn, "Two Interwoven Miracles: The Relational Dimension of Focusing-Oriented Psychotherapy." Unpublished Article.

Remen, Rachel Naomi. *My Grandfather's Blessings*. New York: Riverhead Books, 2000.

Rogers, Carl R. *On Becoming A Person*. Boston: Houghton Mifflin, 1961.

Sander, Louis. *Reflections on Self-Psychology*. Lichtenberg, Joseph and Kaplan, Samuel (editors). The Analytic Press, 1983, pg. 86. Quoted in Preston, Lynn and Shumsky, Ellen, "Toward an Integrative Sensibility." *International Journal of Psychoanalytic Self Psychology*, 8: 309-327, 2013.

Saunders, George. "George Saunder's Advice to Graduates" by Joel Lovell. New York Times.com, July 31, 2013.

Steindl-Rast, Brother David. *Gratefulness, the Heart of Prayer*. New York/Ramsey: Paulist Press, 1984.

Steindl-Rast, Brother David. *A Listening Heart: The Spirituality of Sacred Sensuousness*. New York: Crossroads, 1999.

Steindl-Rast, David. "Spirituality as Common Sense." Iadavaia 21-30.

Steindl-Rast, David. "The Monk in Us." Iadavaia 31-46.

Steindl-Rast, David. "Views of the Cosmos." Iadavaia 65-80.

Steindl-Rast, David. "The God Problem." Iadavaia 92-105.

Steindl-Rast, David. "The Price of Peace." Iadavaia 166-174.

Steindl-Rast, David. "The Great Circle-Dance of the Religions." Retrieved from www. gratefulness.org. (Originally from *The Community of Religions: Voices and Images of the Parliament of the World's Religions.* Teasdale, Wayne and Cairns (editors). Chicago: Continuum Publishing Group, 1996.)

Steindl-Rast, David. "Hymn to the Great Song." Retrieved from www.gratefulness.org. (Part of Michael Stillwater's documentary series from Song Without Borders initiative.)

Steindl-Rast, David. "Word, Silence, and Understanding." Retrieved from www. gratefulness.org. (Originally printed as "Christian Confrontation with Hinduism and Buddhism." *Integral Yoga*, Vol. VI, No. 2. pp. 7-12.)

Tillich Paul. *Dynamics of Faith*. New York: Harper & Rowe, 1957.

Tillich, Paul. *Systematic Theology, Volume 2*. Chicago: University of Chicago Press, 1963.

"The Top Ten Most Influential Therapists of the Past Quarter-Century." *Psychotherapy Networker*, March/April 2007.

Whyte, David. "Faith." *River Flow*. Langley, Washington: Many Rivers Press, 2007.

Winfrey, Oprah. "What Oprah Knows for Sure About Growing Up." *O. The Oprah Magazine*, May 2001.